It Takes a Lot More than Attitude...

To Lead a Stellar Organization

It Takes a Lot More
than Attitude...

To Lead a Stellar Organization

Stever Robbins

Published by Acanthus Publishing
www.acanthuspublishing.com

Acanthus Publishing
a division of
The Ictus Initiative

Library of Congress Cataloging-in-Publication Data

Robbins, Stever.
It takes a lot more than attitude– : to lead a stellar organization / Stever Robbins.
p. cm.
ISBN 0-9754810-0-2
1. Leadership. 2. Executive ability. 3. Chief executive officers. 4. Industrial
management. I. Title.
HD57.7.R627 2004
658.4'092   QBI04-200186

Printed in the United States of America
10 9 8 7 6 5 4 3 2 1

Designed by Charisse L. Brookman
Cover Art by Punchstock/Eyewire
Illustrations by Dan Rosandich

I'd like to dedicate this book to the four greatest friends and mentors a person could hope for:

Marla Schmitter for sparking my vision,

Donald Burnstine for offering my first glimpse of organizations,

Richard Bandler for helping me develop deep insight into the nature of being human, and

Len Schlesinger for giving me the experience of working for and with one of the finest business leaders the human race has ever produced (that would be him).

Contents

Part 1
The Rights and Responsibilities of Being at the Top

Part 2
Leading with Vision—
Getting Things Done through Other People

Part 3
Staying Organized, Focused and Sane

Acknowledgements

This book would never have come to pass without contributions, discussions, and support from hundreds of people. Thank you, my mentors, who have shaped my approach to business and life: Marla Schmitter, Don Burnstine, Richard Bandler, and Len Schlesinger.

In small, growing companies, leadership matters on a daily basis. Thank you, entrepreneurs and executives who have given me valuable lessons of what to do (and sometimes what not to do) as a business leader: Charlie Bachman of Bachman Information Systems; Scott Cook and Tom Proulx of Intuit; Dan Esbensen and Debra Robinson of Touch Technologies, Inc.; Andy McKee and Kevin Sheehan of Hear Music; Rolly Rouse and Tom Ashbrook of BuildingBlocks Interactive; Alec Hudnut of Univesity Access; Robert Jones of Caribiana; and Tony, Matt, Deb, Kaming, Alex, and Stephen of ZEFER Corp.

For brainstorming, late night ponderings, and generally giving great perspectives on business and leadership, thank you my friends and colleagues Marla McDonald, Paula Groves, Justin Miller, Lisa Rogers, Brenda Reiswerg, Liz Kellison, Stephen Carr, and Carol Gignoux.

When it comes to getting out there in the world, I've had the great fortune to work with some great marketing professionals. Thanks, Amy Watson, Tom Phillips, and Ellen Bossert!

Many fine editors have helped me hone my writing over the years. Thanks, Nick Morgan, Laura Tiffany, Karen Spaeder, Teresa Ciulla, and Lori Francisco. And for doing the immense amount of work to create this book, thank you Ictus Initiative—Paige Stover Hague, Mike Black, Charisse Brookman, George Kasparian, and James Richie.

For giving me encouragement, putting up with me when I'm stressed on deadline and doing my best Tasmanian Devil imitation, and generally being there, thank you my partner, Jeffrey Quinlan.

Like any act of communication, writing is a two-way street. All the preparation, learning, and writing makes no difference unless you're out there reading. Thank you for reading.

Stever Robbins
Cambridge, Massachusetts
April 20, 2004

Foreword

If you are an executive in a growing business, juggling day-to-day customer demands, handling the stresses of growth, and needing to develop as a powerful leader at the same time, this book is for you. Stever Robbins tells you how to build an organization, how to master your own development plan, and how to keep yourself sane while doing it.

When you are looking for insight into the leadership fundamentals that make a real difference, it is so very easy to be inundated with questionable theories, complex models, and baffling generalities. Fortunately, Stever Robbins provides us with just the opposite:

- Clear common sense.
- Simple, principle-driven distinctions you can actually work with.
- Specific, actionable approaches to producing real, meaningful results as a leader.

By offering us a readily accessible, easily digestible, and immensely helpful look under the covers of what goes on for a real leader, Stever provides that rarest of perspectives – one which is both philosophically sound, and eminently practical.

Drawing on his decades of work as a leader and executive with over a dozen companies—from start-ups to giants, from super successes to dismal failures—Stever gets us to understand what it really takes for a leader to be successful. In all of the different aspects of leadership responsibility, you get clear, specific, and thoughtful strategies to implement, which are well grounded in the fundamental principles he helps us to understand.

Stever's wealth of experience, both what to do and what not to do, provide a practical basis to his insights and suggestions that just seems to be missing from too many of the 10,000 plus books on leadership available today. Whether he is discussing the development of culture, or the impact of a leader in so many small yet highly meaningful ways, you get the sense that "Yes, I can understand this" and even more importantly, "I can do it!" Even as he expounds on the responsibilities of every leader, his sense of humor and talent for making the complex simple shine through.

If you have leadership responsibilities, or wish to one day soon, now is the time to read this book. Consider the impact that every excellent decision you make has... and know that reading this book—no, studying it would be even more appropriate—will be one of those truly rewarding decisions you will look back on.

I strongly urge you to read this book, and even more importantly to put it to work for you. You, your team, your customers, and your organization will be glad you did.

Steve Lishansky, CEO

Success Dynamics
Concord, Massachusetts
April 18, 2004

Introduction

"We need stronger leadership in this company!" Do you agree? It's the most common complaint I hear from businesspeople, and I hear it everywhere. I even hear it from CEOs, and if CEOs are feeling a leadership void, someone somewhere is missing big-time.

Several years ago, I was coaching a company leader who insisted on spending his time doing everything except leading his company. In frustration, I wrote a letter outlining a CEO's duties and responsibilities and sent a copy to several colleagues to review. They wrote back with questions and a newsletter was born. It led to a presentation, several articles, and regular Question/Answer columns on Entrepreneur.com and *Harvard Business School's Working Knowledge.*

Between people's questions and the issues that surface working with executives, it has become clear that few leaders really understand what their job is, how to be effective in it, and how to do it well. Leadership is fuzzy; we know it when we see it, but we're hard-pressed to define it or teach it. That's because leadership is fundamentally about people. It's about motivating, aligning, and inspiring people to accomplish together something greater than they could do alone. Leading is rooted in emotion, and we don't even teach how to manage our own emotions, much less how to deal with others'.

Business leaders have it even tougher, since they manage processes as well as people. Businesses succeed in part through efficiency. Efficiency comes from analysis, and analysis is easy to teach. So we teach it. And we teach it. And we teach it. And we produce lots of leaders who can run the numbers but aren't so good when it comes to people. Ironically, the numbers can be (and often are) outsourced! A consultant can run numbers, but a consultant can't do the people leadership.

If I've done my job right, however, this book will help *you* do the people side of leadership. I wrote it from a desire to make the people side of leadership accessible. I've collected several articles into book form, added new material, and hopefully produced a useful guide for any leader who wants to get better at their job. In it, you'll find a real exploration of what it means to be a leader and how you can start adopting those skills today. You'll learn to forge a leader/follower relationship with those around you, and keep yourself sane while doing it.

Whether you're seeking to increase your leadership skills in an existing job, entering a new leadership position, or just reading because you're curious, start this book with a commitment to yourself. Commit to using what you learn to help build stronger organizations around you. That's what leaders do, and by opening this book, you've already taken the first step.

Part 1

The Rights and Responsibilities of Being at the Top

"With all due respect sir, wouldn't a simple
CEO suffice?"

Chapter 1
The CEO's Role

"Blessed is he who talks in circles,
for he shall become a big wheel."
— Frank Dane

Admit it. We all feel a touch of awe (or is it jealousy?) when someone has it: the CEO title. It means power, money, and the chance to Be The Boss. It's worthy of awe!

Too bad so few CEOs are good at what they do. Many don't know what their job is, and few of those can pull it off well. It's a simple job—very simple. But it's not at all easy.

More than with any other job, a CEO's *responsibilities* have little to do with their *duties* and *how they're measured.*

A CEO's responsibilities: everything! Whether a one-room shop or a Global 1000, the CEO is responsible for the company's success or failure. Operations, marketing, strategy, financing, creation of company culture, human resources, hiring, firing, compliance with safety regulations, sales, PR, etc.—it all falls on the CEO's shoulders.

3

Without some serious chemical assistance (and a *really* small company), no one could do everything a CEO is responsible for. A CEO's duties are the parts she doesn't delegate. But guess what, even as CEO, some things just can't be delegated. Creating culture, building the senior management team, financing the growth of the company, and, indeed, the delegation itself can only be done by the CEO. Woe betide the CEO who can't do those things well!

The CEO's job description breaks down as follows:

- Set strategy and vision.
- Define and maintain a consistent corporate culture.
- Build effective teams.
- Allocate human and financial resources.

A CEO's main duty is leading: setting strategy and vision

CEOs love to trumpet themselves as strategic geniuses when things go right, but in my experience, the up-front forethought only occasionally existed. Some CEOs delegate it to their team. And yeah, any good strategy will use input from people actually running the company. But the CEO makes the final go/no-go call. Other CEOs delegate strategy to overpriced teams of 26-year-old McStrategy consultants. One Boston-based consulting firm's venture fund is nearly a billion dollars. All that money came from CEOs outsourcing their own job. But the CEO ultimately sets the direction, whether they invented it or took it from others:

- Which markets will the company enter?
- Which competitors will the company take on?
- With what product lines?
- How will the company differentiate itself?

The CEO decides, sets budgets, forms partnerships, and hires a team to steer the company accordingly.

The CEO's second duty is building culture

Even today, people do most of the work in business, and culture affects people. A lot. If a work environment sucks, high performers will leave. They have their pick of places to work, and life is too short to spend it in mediocrity. A great place to work, however, can attract and retain the very best. They'll come by the dozen if they know they'll get up every morning eager to get to work. And guess what—they'll perform better, too!

Culture happens everywhere, but it all starts with the CEO or owner. The culture becomes their personality (or lack thereof) on a grand scale. Every action—or inaction—sends a cultural message. Clothes signal the level of formality. An owner in jeans sets a different tone from the owner who dresses at Neiman's. Who does she talk to? About what? The answers signal who and what is most important. Does she pound people for making mistakes or help them learn? That signals how okay it is to take risks. Even in a five-person company, culture is powerful. Who gets fired, what gets tolerated, and what gets rewarded shape the culture powerfully.

A project team worked weekends launching a multimedia web site on a tight deadline. The owner was on holiday when the site launched. She didn't call to congratulate the team; she wanted to keep her personal life sacred. The team saw it differently: they'd just sacrificed their personal weekends and evenings to meet her deadline. They saw her as saying her personal life was more important than theirs. Next time, they didn't work quite so hard. The culture got slammed, even though that wasn't the CEO's intent. Congratulations on a job well done can motivate a team like nothing else. Silence can demotivate just as quickly.

Team-building is the CEO's #3 duty

The CEO hires, fires, and leads the senior management team. They, in turn, hire, fire, and lead the rest of the organization.

The CEO *must* be able to hire and fire non-performers. She has to keep senior folks from tearing each other's throats out, and she must keep them all working for a common goal. She sets direction by dwelling on the strategy and vision at every opportunity. It's the strategy that sets direction. With clear direction, people can rally together and really accomplish something.

Direction setting is wicked powerful! In 1991, at Intuit's new employee orientation, CEO Scott Cook presented his vision of Intuit as the center of computerized personal finance. Intuit had 120 employees and one product. I laughed. A decade later, it's a multi-billion-dollar company with thousands of employees and dozens of products. Worldwide, it is the winner in personal finance, bar none. Now Scott's laughing. Every employee had that vision down cold, and they made choice after choice that moved Intuit to become that vision in reality.

If vision is *where* the company is going, values are *how* it gets there. Values say what is and isn't acceptable behavior. Values come from example. Top managers broadcast values with every action, decision, and reaction. They choose to deliver late on a customer contract to meet a certain quality level? They've just proclaimed that quality is important. Giving a lukewarm reception to a team's heroic recovery when they could have avoided the problem altogether sends a message about prevention versus damage control. People take their cues about interpersonal values—trust, honesty, openness—from actions at the top as well.

Capital allocation is the CEO's #4 duty

Money, money, money. The top dog determines where it goes. Is it used to pay salaries, or to invest in a self-congratulatory billboard in a nearby office park? It's the CEO's call. If she's doing her job, she funds projects that support the strategy, and kills money-losing projects or projects that don't support the strategy. She ponders major expenditures, and manages the firm's capital. If the company can't use each dollar spent to produce at least $1 of shareholder value, she decides when to return money to the investors. Even if a CEO doesn't view herself as a financial person, at the end of the day, her money decisions make or break the company.

Chapter 2
Total Scrutiny of Your Every Move
Leadership Under a Magnifying Glass

> *"When people are free to do as they please, they usually imitate each other."*
>
> — Eric Hoffer

"Why don't my people just do what I say?" is a common refrain among top managers. Life would be so much easier, they imagine, if only "people" would "get it." Er, hello? Isn't that the top manager's job? To make sure that "people" "get it?"

If you're a top manager, you must own your power, or in this case, the genetically-determined effect you have on everyone beneath you. You see, values and direction depend so heavily on upper management because we're all primates. No, really. We're hard-wired to live in a hierarchy, and we get our cues from the baboon at the top. Employees probably *are* doing what you say; you just don't realize you're broadcasting proclamations you don't intend. It's the little things that have the biggest impact.

Remember when you were a front-line employee? Your managers' actions were relentlessly scrutinized. A late arrival, a smile, or a nod could introduce chaos at the water cooler: "She smiled. Does that mean she approves of the report I wrote last week, or does that mean she intends to fire me and is satisfied with her choice of replacement?" One business owner was looking over his marketing department's latest campaign. He frowned at a storyboard before strolling away.

Oops. Bad idea. The team saw the frown, scrapped the campaign, and spent the weekend reworking everything from the ground up. When he found out, he was flabbergasted. He never thought a simple frown would change the team's direction.

Reactions to people's work send signals. Remember this! Frowning or smiling, a head nod or shake all send a message. If you're the one smiling, think about the message you may have sent, and say or do whatever it takes to make sure your audience knows your intent. If you're the one being frowned at, have a conversation and find out what's really happening. It's a sad day when a boss has gas and a great employee starts circulating their resume because they misinterpreted an after-lunch grimace.

Words matter too. A joke may not be a joke. A small consulting company's Managing Director smiled and quipped, "Remember, if you're not here Sunday, don't bother coming in Monday." He was smiling. Everyone knew he was joking. And as one team member later shared, "I felt like I had to come in Sunday. Sure, he was joking. But he's the Managing Director. Maybe it's not 100% a joke."

Leadership happens by example

Was the Managing Director in the office on Sunday? Of course. And so he insured everyone would consider weekend appearances required. Actions trump everything else when it comes to communicating priorities. Period. The Managing Director really did care deeply that his people have an outside life, and said so on many occasions. But his coming in on weekends spoke louder than words and people followed his lead, rushing headlong into burnout.

What isn't done also matters

Whole sitcoms have been written about people (usually men) who forget to say "Happy Anniversary." A simple forgotten thought can lead to a full half-hour of zany antics, hard feelings, and Hollywood angst. Silence can be as powerful as action. Messages sent by what *didn't* get said or done are often overlooked until way too late. The vacationing business owner who neglected to give her team congratulations wasn't asking "What message am I not sending?" Her attention was just elsewhere. Forgotten messages are tricky to anticipate because there's nothing there to examine! But knowing what people expect makes it possible to speak loudly with silence.

So what do people expect?

People expect acknowledgement. Praise them when they're doing well! Otherwise, they won't feel valued. And when they don't feel valued, they slack off, big-time. *How* to praise differs from person to person. Some people need public proclamations when they do well. Give 'em "Employee of the Month." Others need a quiet mention in the office once in a while. Give that to them, too. Find out what works for each person (you can ask), and make sure you let them know how much you appreciate their work.

People expect to know when they're doing poorly. Well, okay, most people just want to know they did great. So that's the only message some managers give, even when the person's losing it, big-time. Then at some point, the manager gets fed up and fires them. It happens all the time, and everyone loses. The employee feels misled and stabbed in the back; after all, they were told they were doing great. The manager is demoralized by their own cowardice.

The company gets sued. And everyone else gets two takeaways: that sub par performance is acceptable, and that firing is seemingly arbitrary without a chance to make things right. As difficult as it can be to give negative feedback, not giving it can be disastrous.

People expect common courtesy. Sometimes, it seems courtesy has almost vanished. But when it vanishes totally, especially from a company owner, its absence communicates a lack of respect. Say "Please" or "Thank you" with a smile and direct eye contact; it takes only a second, and lets someone know they're important. If you're too busy for courtesy, you're telling people they aren't important enough to care about. And how many people are going to care about the agenda of a boss who doesn't care about them?

People expect to be listened to. It's amazing how much commitment is produced by simply having people be part of a decision. If you make decisions behind closed doors, people read that as anything from indifference to outright distrust. I have worked with companies where senior managers are very open with their big decisions, and other companies where "we can't tell them that" is a common refrain. Contrary to popular belief, open decisions don't seem to bring on a rain of fire, while the "we can't tell them that" attitude often loses the respect of people down the line. When involvement is missing, the message of distrust is loud and clear.

People expect to know the bad news. Not sharing bad news sends the message that everything is fine. It's easy to keep bad news quiet, for fear of hurting morale. But if the news is really bad, word gets around anyway and then morale still drops, but the managers (who are officially towing the good-news line) can't even discuss what's happening openly. Sharing bad news honestly and framing it as a reason to rally builds a team instead of breaking it down. Shared challenge is the stuff of bonding.

A great business leader knows his impact

Matsushita, one of history's most successful businessmen, knew the impact he had on everyone around him. As this story shows[1], he even appreciated the messages conveyed by what he *didn't* do.

The father of a $75 billion empire, Matsushita was revered in Japan with nearly as much respect and reverence as was the Emperor. And he was just as busy.

One day, Matsushita was to eat lunch with his executives at a local Osaka restaurant. Upon his entrance, people stopped to bow and acknowledge this great man. Matsushita honored the welcome and sat at a table selected by the manager.

Matsushita ate only half of his meal. He asked for the chef, who appeared in an instant, shaken and upset. The Great One nodded and spoke: "I felt that if you saw I had only eaten half of my meal, you would think I did not like the food or its preparation. Nothing could be less true. The food and your preparation of it were excellent. I am just old and can not eat as much as I used to. I wanted you to know that and to thank you personally."

---

[1] I am uncertain as to the origin of this story and cannot give appropriate credit to a source. (E-mail me if you know the source.)

Concrete next steps: how you can deal with the magnifying glass

Leaders live under a magnifying glass. That's just life. A few simple guidelines can help manage the scrutiny:

1. Use a daily "Magnifying Review" to reduce surprises. Take note of everyone you did and didn't contact and ask what message you sent. It will take about five minutes and you'll be able to catch political messes before they have a chance to take hold.

2. Use the scrutiny to send a message. At the start of the week, choose a message you want to communicate by example. Spend a moment or two identifying exactly where you can send the message, and how you have to behave to send it. Then do it.

3. Ask what you didn't say. During your daily review, ask who you *didn't* contact, but who might have expected it (you may not know who at first, but over time, you'll learn). What message did the lack of contact send? What message will rumors of what you *did* do send to those who didn't see/talk to you?

4. Review company systems. To make sure you're sending the same message as your company, do a yearly check-up. Review your compensation plan: what does it say about company goals? What does it encourage? Discourage? Review your decision-making and feedback processes. Ask yourself if you're omitting anyone or anything in those areas.

Chapter 3
Gaining Traction with a Powerful Strategic Plan

*"An organization that is strong
and stable and is ready to commit
time, money, and patience will be
more apt to reap rewards than the
quick-hitting opportunist."*

— Richard Miller

You can't simply communicate the direction and values of a company and expect them to happen. Those directions have to turn into action, and it's management that does the turning. Managers design systems, set goals, track progress, and generally make sure things get done. Both leaders and managers are needed to create a high-performing organization: know where to go, and how to get there.

A lot can go wrong. If the leadership at the top is weak, the organization can stagger in circles, incoherent and directionless. Weak management and a weak organization wastes time and money, duplicates effort, and produces far too much (or too little) paperwork. But even strong management and strong leadership can dissolve into chaos without a tight connection translating the leadership direction into management systems. *You use the strategic plan to connect leadership and management and give your business traction.*

The strategic plan defines a do-able chunk of the next year's journey toward the ultimate vision. A good plan takes into account how much progress the company can make in the next year, where it is now, and how best to cover the territory in between.

Leadership sets the destination

One company's vision statement lays out the company's purpose, vision, and values:

"Our Business is the design and manufacture of impenetrable widgets for renewable energy source control plants. We aspire to become a leading worldwide player where customers love our products and service, and where these are provided at consistently good quality and a fair price."

Sounds like a great vision. It tells product development what to make, displays values of customer-orientation and quality, and even lets us know the company's intended markets. It sounds inspirational, and like most leadership documents, it's timeless; the company could be living this vision right now, or it could be hopelessly mired, years away from making the vision real. Of course, it could also be that this vision is just a bunch of nice-sounding words scribbled on a boardroom wall, with no link to the business whatsoever. The challenge is making sure it becomes real.

Ideally, the vision drives strategy. Most management goals serve a higher-level goal. The sales goal "land 10 new clients" is part of the higher goal, "increase market share by 5%." The company's strategy is the highest-level management goal. Its guidance comes straight from the vision and mission of the company—which is where leadership resides.

Well-scoped goals drive success

The strategic plan can't get all the way to the vision, of course. It can only get part way there. That "part way" is the goal the plan sets out for the year.

The best goals set the organization up for success. Yeah, yeah, setting "stretch" goals is all the rage. But people can be stretched too far. In the Middle Ages, they used a rack and called it torture. In the 21st century, they use a clock and call it "productivity." Achievable plans are realistic about what's possible in a year. Productivity isn't about blind action; it's about ruthless focus on the few goals that make the most difference. Ruthless overwork on low-value initiatives just generates really rapid garbage.

Fortunately, nature's given us a built-in governor, even if we usually ignore it: productivity goes down under too much stress or too little sleep. So it only makes sense to scope do-able goals. If it will take 283 initiatives to reach this year's goals, the goals must be changed, because they're hopeless. People will be too stressed to do a good job, and besides, consider 283 status meetings each week… it's simply too horrible to think about.

Assessment gives the starting place

Knowing where you're going is the first step. You can't navigate to your destination without knowing where you're starting. "Go West Young Man" gets you someplace very different if you start in Miami instead of New York. So you have to know where you are before you can chart a course. Strategic assessment gives the starting point. Once you know that, you can choose a route.

A lot of people only look at high-level financial measures to assess where they are: market share, revenue, and profit goals are common. But those are only one set of measurements.

Aligning an organization demands richer internal and external assessments:

- What organizational capabilities exist?
- How is the company positioned against competitors?
- Are partnerships in place? the right ones?
- Does the organization attract and retain the right employees?
- Does the culture support those employees?
- Do profitable customers stick around?
- Does the financial strategy deliver money when needed?
- Are product and service actually being delivered?

A good assessment has a mix of objective measurements and subjective judgment calls. You'll want to consult people up and down throughout the organization in figuring out where the organization is right now.

Make your plan stronger by including organizational learning

Okay, so you've got a starting point and a destination. You're ready to chart a course and form the strategic plan. But which plan? A straight line might look attractive, but hidden roadblocks may take you down a different route. Choosing a strategic route is a simple decision with enormous consequences. One tweak in the plan can change the outcome drastically. With that much at stake, strategic planning deserves to include some organizational learning.

No one wants to repeat past mistakes and everyone likes to repeat successes. Most organizations learn a lot, but the learning gets lost.

When Intuit launched the Quicken Visa Card, the software-only company learned that a credit card business is a whole different ball of wax. The business's infrastructure was revamped multiple times to make use of lessons learned about reliability, security, and customer service.

When putting together the next year's strategic plan, have people spend some time reviewing the prior year's. What worked? What didn't? What assumptions did the company make that were flat-out wrong? Which assumptions were right? What did the team think they could do well, but couldn't? What did the team *think* they couldn't do, but could? Taking time to understand the evolving capabilities and context of a business pays for itself in multiples when you use the understanding to drive revisions of your strategic plan.

Plans hand off from leadership into management

With a solid destination, starting point, and route, it's finally time to propagate plans throughout the organization. The transition from leadership to management is in full swing. Now, the managers get to take the ball and run with it. All the standard planning rules apply:

- Have lots of measurable milestones.
- Schedule regular re-planning sessions.
- Know the critical paths.
- Communicate success criteria clearly.
- Coordinate between different groups.
- Monitor the plan and adjust as necessary.

Leadership remains important

When the plan is in action, the leadership vision is on its way to reality. But the job of the leader is far from over! Now your job shifts to keeping a powerful presence, reminding people of the company's ultimate destination, values, and reason for existing.

People will get de-motivated; you re-inspire them. Plans will drift or the world will change; you call for re-examining whether the organization is still on course. You provide the stability of direction and values that free everyone else to make it happen.

Even if the world is wildly different than expected, sound strategic planning will provide the map that aligns an organization behind the leader's vision. An aligned, energized organization is more likely to reach the vision, and it will be more fun and more motivating along the way. And at the end of the day, our lives and work are lived in the journey, not the destination.

Putting it into action: linking your leadership to management

Do the people in your company share a common idea of the business's direction? If not, choose a direction and start going for it!

Look around at the initiatives and projects that are under way. Do they all have a clear link to your company's vision/mission? If not, fix them.

Do people seem overworked? Do the research to discover whether goals are poorly scoped, whether the plans to reach those goals are simply bad plans, or whether productivity is suffering from plain old overload. Incorporate that learning into your next planning session.

The next time you start planning, ask yourself whether you know your goals and your current situation, measured along all relevant external and internal dimensions.

Above all, think, then jump. Planning is important, and so is execution. Most of us prefer one or the other, and we get mired in endless plans or senseless execution. Really think about yourself and your organization and make sure you're striking the right balance. A week of planning is more valuable than a year of action in the wrong direction.

Chapter 4
Defining Corporate Culture: What's Visible

"It is only shallow people who do not judge by appearances. The true mystery of the world is the visible, not the invisible."

— *Oscar Wilde*

A big part of your job will be defining culture. Cultures appear the moment you have more than one person in a room (depending on the person, it sometimes doesn't even take two). The group quietly conspires to write unwritten rules. Habits form. Guidelines appear, telling what's right and what's not. Next come dress codes, shared mythology, and even decision-making. Quietly the definition of proper behavior comes into being. Before you know it, even a three-person group can create enough dysfunction to keep Dr. Phil busy for an entire season.

Culture is soft. It's slippery. It's hard-to-define. But themes arise again and again when people praise or slam their culture. Those themes are your keys in shaping your culture deliberately, instead of leaving it to the group's mercy.

Dress code is a visible signal of culture. Scott Cook, centi-millionaire founder of Intuit, came to work virtually every day in casual clothes and a windbreaker. Intuit's culture was informal, with open communication and very little politics. Computer culture, in particular, has been very informal, and some top performers will turn down jobs if they have to wear a suit or work in an environment that feels too formal.

At the other end of the spectrum, many bankers and lawyers wear a full, freshly pressed navy suit every day, even if they won't be seeing clients. The dress code sets a tone of professionalism, and typically, everyone in the office wears a suit and tie.

Dress code matters because it's visible. New employees, clients, and suppliers all get the message. Two consulting firms gave competing presentations for a six-figure contract. After the presenters left, one decision-maker turned to the other and said, "I liked the second group much better. They were all wearing suits. They were much more professional." Really dumb decision-making on the client's part, but the consulting firm knew that dress counted as much as their content.

In my experience, "professional" means a narrower range of behavior. In professional environments, emotional displays are more subdued. The range of acceptable behavior is smaller. Even the clothes restrict extreme movements. Everything seems under control, implying that results are, too. In fields like finance, where clients want reassurance they'll get the outcome they want, an impression of control is vital. Besides, narrower ranges of behavior are easier to manage; you don't have to master as many situations.

Creative environments often have much more flamboyant dress codes. More visual styles imply anything could happen! That's just what you want when you're looking for an outside-the-box ad campaign that will turn your brand into an immortal cultural phenomenon.

Your dress code affects who will work for you, who will buy your products, and how "out-of-the-box" your employees will act. As I write this, "disruptive innovation" and "revolutionary change" are fads of the day. If you want continuous disruption, mandatory suits[1] and set working hours may not be the way.

Space is a visible sign of culture, too

Your space sends messages, just like your people. If everyone sits in a newsroom-style wide-open room where communication is just a shout away, you'll have a very different environment from banks of cubicles or from individual offices with doors that close.

Space affects morale. Attractive spaces are uplifting. Ugly spaces depress. "Feng shui" is an entire Chinese art of directing the flow of chi (life energy) to bring out the best in a space. Whether or not chi's the thing, a nicely designed space can dramatically affect your mood. Most workplaces range from neutral to ugly. Cubicles almost always guarantee "ugly," and since most people have no design sense, occupant-designed offices can be just as bad.

The colors in most workplaces—beige, taupe, and a slightly off-green—are pleasant. The artwork, "Still Life with Flowers #234," is… pleasant. The layout, offices around the windows, cubicles in the center, is… pleasant. Nothing depressing there. Sure, it has so little personality that people feel like faceless cogs in an uncaring world, but hey, at least no one's offended. Isn't that pleasant?

---

[1] Let's be honest, though, we *like* mandatory suits. None of us want out-of-the-box thinkers around. We want people who come up with out-of-the-box solutions while communicating, behaving, and proposing firmly inside our comfort zones.

A technology strategy consulting startup began in a large loft. With no money for a build-out, they had students from the local design school design funky partitions, and a cool paint job, and chose inexpensive stylish furniture. They offered local sculptors space to display artwork on a rotating basis. The result: a funky, unique space. Job candidates would beg to work someplace so cool. Beige might have been "safer," but style actively attracted good people.

Space is more than just aesthetic

Style counts, but function counts too. The company's wide-open space was pretty, but disastrous when people needed quiet thinking space. When designing your space, guide its creation by asking questions about how it will be used:

- Does the space let people communicate? Newsrooms are chaotic, wide-open spaces. Communication is a breeze—yell. Individual offices are the other extreme—informal communication is reserved for the lunchroom.

- Does the space permit isolation when needed for thinking? Closing the door is great for concentration... as long as there's a door.

- Can people move around easily? Can they find each other? Do project teams sit together, or do functional groups sit together?

- Is there room for groups to gather when needed? Do groups have to schedule the one conference room a week in advance, or can they plop down on the couch in front of the whiteboard for an impromptu brainstorming session?

In some companies, space reflects hierarchy. The Big Boss has a corner office. A huge corner office, on the 300th floor. As you go down the hierarchy, offices get smaller, they move from window views to inside views, and eventually bottom out at the secretary's open-air desk next to the bank of cubicles for the masses. Oddly, it often seems in such organizations there's an inverse relationship between office size and the occupant's actual need for space. Most engineers would kill for the unused wall space in a hierarchical CEO's office.

Organizing your space around hierarchy can be dangerous. You get people jostling for pecking order instead of getting stuff done. When a window office is a major indicator of status, you're letting your space stifle your organization. If you run out of window offices, you can't show a valued employee they're important. When windows mean status, gold stars and handshakes won't cut it. In a hundred-person company, office space was a major currency. A top performer left when the window office promised to him was given to a new hire by accident. He didn't really care about the window, but he sure cared about the respect and status the window represented.

Sometimes executive offices are clustered together or on a different floor. Physically isolated, it's easy for top management to lose touch. One facilities manager made sure the executive suite had flawless infrastructure so the top brass wouldn't notice when he fell down managing the rest of the facilities. I recommend physical mixing—it makes it easier to keep vision and values alive. If you're immersed in your company's culture, you'll impact it as a matter of course.

As a company grows and evolves, you can use space to signal major cultural trends. One young company was funded on credit cards. They used desks made of doors and filing cabinets, offices buried behind stacks of paper in rooms sublet from insurance companies, and three offices split among four floors. The space screamed: "We're all creating this new business together." Another well-funded company started in elegant space fit for the Fortune 100. The space gently whispered, "We're a huge, successful company." Alas, the entrepreneurs listened. They talked as if they were already great successes and proudly strutted through the offices, only developing the lean-and-mean discipline needed for a successful company when they'd wasted their initial investment.

Space and dress code are two ways of affecting culture by changing what can be seen from the outside. In the next chapter, we'll explore the hidden elements of culture.

Chapter 5
Defining Corporate Culture: What's Invisible

"Listen, or your tongue will make you deaf."

— *Native American Proverb*

Dress hip or wear a suit. Have a beautiful, character-filled space or live in a sea of pleasant beige. Those things matter. But no matter how much you tweak the external, your culture will live or die based on how you treat your people.

Decision-making is where culture shows up, big-time. Your decisions signal the values of the company, and the very way you make decisions speaks volumes about the culture you're creating.

A software company had a history of shipping low-quality product to make their quarterly numbers. The staff became demoralized, and the CEO announced that in the future, ship dates would be slipped as needed to get quality. Less than a month later, a project team was feeling pressure to ship, despite known poor quality levels. The team leader decided to ship the product, budgeting for a recall, rather than risk hurting quarterly numbers. The CEO, who knew of the situation, did nothing to stop it. Loud and clear, the message was sent: quality doesn't matter, but ship date does.

When values collide and you're forced to choose, your decisions broadcast what's important and what isn't. Over time, these values become embedded in the culture. Our software CEO could say, "value trumps quarterly numbers," but when the heat was on, he couldn't rewrite his decisions to reflect those values. The more he didn't rewrite his decisions, the more the culture didn't become quality-driven. Funny how that works.

If you want to create a culture with certain values, think long and hard about the decisions affected by those values. It's the values conflicts that set the culture; if you can have both ship date and quality, you're not sending any messages. But if you have to choose between the two, the one you choose nudges your culture more in that direction. If you spend time in advance mentally rehearsing values conflicts, you'll be better able to send the messages you want to send with your decisions.

Common Values That Drive Organizational Behavior

- "Do right by the customer."
- Treat each other as if we're family.
- Crush the competition.
- Reward and promote solely for merit.
- Deliver the lowest cost product.
- Treat all peers, employees, suppliers, and customers with respect.
- Provide a satisfying, stimulating place to work.
- Get away with anything we possibly can.
- Buyer beware.
- Ongoing contribution is needed to justify employment.
- Produce a good return for shareholders.
- Deliver quality products.
- Show profitable quarters.
- Dominate all markets we compete in.
- A fair day's pay for a fair day's work.
- Be a good corporate citizen.

Broadcasting values is only half of how you can use decisions to shape culture. *How* you make decisions sends powerful messages. If you involve others and genuinely listen to them, you'll be promoting a culture of participation. This might be just the culture for a manufacturing company depending on all employees to help drive improvement efforts. A group that must make split second decisions under pressure, such as a military unit, might not afford the luxury of participation. If that's you, top-down command-and-control may be the culture you want to build. Just be sure that top-down decision-making is accompanied by genuine listening to information from the bottom. Otherwise, those decisions may ignore important information, and even the world's most brilliant minds will make dumb decisions if they're missing information.

Participative decision-making is hard! It means listening, when all of us so like to talk. You may think you're listening and persuading when, in fact, you're trampling opposition. I facilitated a strategic planning session where the executive team was brimming with great ideas. The CEO spoke last, at double anyone else's volume, and presented his full analysis, recommendations, and conclusions. He just wanted to give input, but the team visibly shut down and took his word as law. People defer to the senior person in the room, period. If you're it, and you deliver a full argument in a loud voice, don't expect to hear any opposition. But don't fool yourself into believing it's because your idea is brilliant; you may just be intimidating.

Occasionally have a third party watch you in a meeting and let you know if you're as inclusive as you wish. If you're brave, have them track your ideas vs. others', and note which get finalized. If you get your way 90% of the time, congratulate yourself on your stellar strategic thinking capabilities. Then slap yourself silly for wasting your team's time, salaries, and abilities.

If you're dominating your team, gag yourself for a few meetings and notice what happens. Just sit quietly, observe, and implement the team's decisions. Let go of the need for the best quality decision, and instead watch for the best *decision-making process*. Notice how your participation changes things. Once you get yourself out of the way, you'll truly open the doors to a culture of participation. (Note: If you have trouble staying quiet, use a real gag. You can, you know. You're the boss—who are *they* to criticize *your* fashion accessories?)

You buy culture with pay

Would you believe—people do what you pay them for? Bizarre, but true. Any shaping of culture must include a close look at what gets rewarded and how. A large manufacturer wanted to transfer its "best practice" from one plant to another. As we delved into why it wasn't happening, we found the culture was fighting back. You see, this company prided itself on breakthrough technology. Their bonuses were given for inventing new ways of doing things. The bonuses worked! The company was chock full of creative, bright people creating breakthrough technology.

When you pay people to innovate, however, the last thing they want to spend their time doing is adopting other people's ideas. Au contraire, they want to spend their time out-creating the other people. The company refused to alter their pay structure. We were informed in no uncertain terms that the bonus structure worked so well, it was forbidden territory. So people kept doing what they were paid for. The company guaranteed that innovative ideas that gave mediocre results would win out over proven brilliance if it came from outside.

In this case, pay was money but it isn't always that way. Vacation time, promotions, benefits, promotions, status, and promotions are all kinds of payment. Notice a pattern? Good. Because one thing people are hypersensitive to is who's on top and who's not. When you promote someone, you're signaling that what they were doing was Really Important. You're also signaling everyone who you didn't promote that their contribution wasn't quite as good.

If you reward longevity, you'll gradually assemble a company full of stable lifers. If you reward bottom-line results and little else, you'll end up with a results-at-all-cost culture. Just remember that people do more of what they're doing when they get a reward. So don't just reward when you notice the right outcomes; make sure you're rewarding the right outcomes *being reached the right way*. Otherwise, you could be getting great results for the wrong reasons. As Enron and a host of others found in the early 2000s, that kind of monkey business eventually comes back to haunt you.

Blame or Learning? Two very different cultures

We all make mistakes. The higher we are, the more we can successfully blame others and no one will contradict us (at least not to our face). But everyone else has a harder time deflecting when things go wrong. How you deal with mistakes will determine how willing people are to take risks, and how much you'll hear the truth, versus hearing only good news, even when what's happening isn't so good.

There's certainly a common attitude that says, "produce results or you're fired." As I write this in early 2004, one of TV's most popular shows is "The Apprentice," where we can watch billionaire Donald Trump point his finger and say, "You're fired." It's a powerfully attractive image, especially to those of us who crave power. While it's an appealing Tough Hero image, in practice, you'll get a lot more mileage by adopting an attitude of "make mistakes, but learn from them, or you're fired."

The more you treat mistakes as chances to learn, the more people will be willing to push the edge of the envelope. That's the edge where brilliance will happen ... sometimes. Sure, there will be flops, but the gems can make up for it. If 3M had punished failure, they may never have turned a failed glue into Post-It pads, now a multi-decade, multi-billion-dollar cash cow.

Of course, you still have to beware of failures caused by repeated ineptitude combined with a lack of learning. Sometimes, failure really does come from incompetence. But before you fire for failure, consider what that will do to your culture, and make sure that you've given learning a chance. More on that in Chapter 7.

Between decision-making, pay, and how you treat mistakes, you have all the levers you need to design and powerfully adjust your culture.

Chapter 6
Create a Culture Where Individual Contribution and Team Success is Celebrated

"Corporations are social organizations, the theater in which men and women realize or fail to realize purposeful and productive lives."

— Peter Rena

Do you get enough praise and recognition when you do a good job? If you're like most people, you'll answer "No." Yet giving praise when it's deserved can be an important piece of building a high-performing organization. Although our culture seems founded in punishment, the most effective learning happens by highlighting and encouraging the best in people, not by punishing the worst. If used well, the carrot is mightier than the stick[1].

Many companies search for ways to show appreciation publicly, and a company that does it well is on its way to being a great place to work. Let's go

---

[1] For a wonderful overview of how rewards work, see *Don't Shoot the Dog* by Karen Pryor.

one step further and ask: how can we create a day-to-day work environment which gives that recognition?

Public appreciation is nice, but it doesn't happen often, and can have a "special event" aura. I find people need an ongoing boost. Appreciation isn't a special event—it is part of our day-to-day living.

How do you recognize employees for doing a great job? Believe it or not, one of the best strategies is also the simplest: compliment people. We're not talking some huge production. When you drop by someone's desk, tell them how great their work has been. That's all there is to it. A casual comment and the deed is done.

Compliments are more likely to be heard if you frame them in terms of your reaction to their achievement, rather than their actions alone. For example, "I found your analysis last Tuesday was well thought-out. It helped me choose our next steps." If you say "Good job," someone with low self-esteem can disregard the compliment, thinking, "It could have been much better." But no one can argue with "Here's the value I got from what you did."

Use compliments carefully because people do more of what they're praised for. The manager who says, "Gee, I loved your presentation" to rescue someone's ego after a mind-numbing three-hour informationless mumble-fest is in big trouble. Happily believing they did a good job, the presenter will try it again. If others overhear the compliment, they might try mumbling too. So make sure your praise is sincere. In 1978, someone complimented my Uncle on his wonderful Thanksgiving turnip surprise. The entire family is still suffering the consequences. *Shudder.*

True, credible, tactful compliments work best. "It seemed to me they decided to buy when your presentation linked our product features to their needs."

There are lots of opportunities to show appreciation:

- People stay late to meet a deadline (especially if the schedule slip page isn't their fault.)

- An employee rearranges their personal life to accommodate work.

- Someone goes beyond their job description to do something that benefits the company, culture, or community.

- A person spots a future problem and fixes it before it becomes serious.

Appreciation comes in many forms and price points:

- Taking the team for a spontaneous lunch outing, your treat.

- A day off and road trip someplace fun (not expensive, just fun.)

- The fun new software your programmers want, even though it has no business value.

- Listening to opinions and considering that when you disagree, they may be right.

- Put huge stuffed animals on their chair to hug them when they arrive in the morning (Not advised for environments with high macho factors.)

- Movie gift certificates.

- Two tickets to a fabulous event.

- Ending meetings on time, showing respect for peoples' time.

- Not scheduling Monday meetings before 10 am, or Friday meetings after 3 pm.

Putting it into action: appreciating good people

- Think about the people you work with. Identify several things they do on a daily basis and simply thank them.

- Figure out one or two great things your team has done. Take them out to a nice lunch just to show your appreciation.

- And remember, this works in your personal life as well.

Chapter 7
Taking Risks and Learning from Mistakes

"Far better is it to dare mighty things, to win glorious triumphs even though checkered by failure than to take rank with those poor spirits who neither enjoy much nor suffer much because they live in the grey twilight that knows neither victory nor defeat."

— Theodore Roosevelt

It's a tired refrain in business, "We wish people would take more risks and think outside the box." Uh-huh. Face the Truth. We're afraid to admit mistakes for a good reason: culturally, we don't tolerate mistakes. Since first grade, we've been scolded, punished, given poor grades, passed over for promotion, ostracized, and belittled for our mistakes. As I write this, we're heading into a whopping third season of "American Idol." As usual, it begins with a countrywide mockery of talentless pop-star wannabes. Talentless? For sure. But at least they had the courage to take a risk in front of 250 million people. Their reward? Public ridicule, often reducing contestants to tears. Are they going to be leading the pack of risk-takers in the future? Would you?

Sure, some people say mistakes are okay. A well meaning, understanding person—usually from the Human Potential movement—says in a soft, caring voice, "It's not a mistake, it's a learning opportunity." Two days later, the team member who *didn't* make the mistake is promoted to team leader. It was a learning opportunity, all right. The learning was, "Don't screw up, follow the rules, don't make mistakes and you'll have a career."

Society's message is, "Don't admit mistakes or bad things will happen." If you want people in your organization taking risks, you have to make it safe, even desirable, for them to move outside their comfort zone.

The organization must support risk-taking

Look first to your rewards. Most organizations reward outcomes: sell the most, get promoted; meet your ship date, get a bonus; meet your earnings projections, get an analyst's stamp of approval. The rewards come from reaching an outcome, no matter how it was reached. Imagine Laurie, a shoe salesperson for OutcomeCo. Laurie's sales tactics work on just 1% of the customers. Fortunately, the territory is flush with that 1%, so meeting quarterly targets is a breeze. Laurie is motivated to milk the 1%, rather than take risks to capture the other 99%.

> **"** People do what they're paid
> for, so pay them to learn. **"**

And why should Laurie take risks? Risk-taking by its nature misses targets much of the time. The solution is to reward *the learning process* as well as the targets. Imagine LearningCo, where the bonus is based on helping the company move faster toward its goals by gathering useful information, developing better ways of doing things, or identifying what not to do again (mistakes).

In LearningCo, Laurie is rewarded for capturing the 1%, but is also rewarded for noticing market trends, trying cool new sales tactics that don't work—no doubt involving unicycles, French horns, and a powdered wig—and inventing cool new products that may someday take over the market.

People do what they're paid for, so pay them to learn. Add personal risk-taking plans to yearly reviews. Ask, "Are you taking enough risks? How can I help you take more?" Applaud in public (and in private!) when someone fails at something wildly, audaciously new. Celebrate whoever has the wackiest new ideas. Otherwise, time spent thinking outside the box is also time spent thinking outside the bonus structure. Given the choice between outside-the-box poverty and inside-the-BMW business-as-usual, don't be surprised when people choose the BMW.

It's hard to reward learning in an outcome-based culture; you need real conviction. Are you ready to pad schedules with time for failures, experimentation, and rework? Could you give a larger bonus to someone who learned and failed than to someone who reached an important outcome through sheer luck? And if so, are you up to the task of making sure everyone understands that the learning is what you are rewarding?

A software company gave their flagship product's manager a Hawaiian vacation when the product shipped. The flagship product accounted for 70% of the company's revenue, so the manager was given unlimited budget and staff to insure success. Why should he learn? He could just commandeer more resources. Other projects were cannibalized without notice for the flagship project, so they learned to streamline development and ship with limited resources. Taken at face value, it sounds reasonable to reward the flagship manager more than the other managers, yet he contributed much less to the organization's ongoing strength and capability. By not rewarding the *other* managers for their learning in a difficult situation, they eventually lost many good performers.

39

One-on-one support is also needed for risk-taking

Once the organization structures support risk-taking, you have to encourage the behaviors daily. When someone's pushing the edge of their thinking, be excited! Ask questions to push them further. Daily brainstorming, questioning assumptions, and experimentation must become "*de rigeur.*" When someone surfaces an idea that could lead to great learning, keep it alive by giving them time and resources to pursue the idea further.

> **"** Time spent thinking outside-the-box is also time spent thinking outside-the-bonus-structure. **"**

If your culture doesn't allow mistakes, the gossip circles can be vicious. If you hear someone making fun of another person's mistake or missed targets, challenge the gossip. Ask "Was the mistake because they were trying something new?"

This is a change that has to happen at the grassroots. You have to get people talking about out-of-the-box thinking. When they first hear a novel idea, people will retreat to what's familiar. "If we did that, we'd get fired and lose our bonuses." The fears and excuses you hear reveal your organization's unique neuroses and phobias of risk-taking. You need to be countering these phobias by asking, "What would have to happen for you to feel safe enough go out on a limb and try?" or "If you knew your career was completely safe, do you think that idea would be worth trying?" Oh, yes. When they answer, listen to what they say. You'll learn a lot about how to help people shift their mindset.

Have learning reviews, and start with facts

Contrary to popular belief, learning doesn't just happen. It takes reflection and consideration. Even for those of us who know that, it's easy to spend a couple decades repeating our own personal dysfunction until something jolts us to really look at our behavior, identify the patterns, and change it.

In organizations, reflection comes from project reviews. When a major milestone comes and goes, get the team together to reflect on what made it possible (or impossible) to meet the milestone. Have them turn their observations into guidelines that can apply to future projects. Even if your culture is generally supportive, you'll get the most out of a review if you keep it all about the facts, not the people.

Learning comes from examining what did and didn't happen, not assigning blame or recognition. Personal commitment only becomes key when the team begins exploring the future. Once learning becomes commonplace, people may become comfortable owning their part in what happens. Until then, a focus on the people just makes them defensive.

Because, you see, at project reviews, each person—and usually the whole team—will assume their own behavior was flawless. Like Martha Stewart at arraignment, everyone feels they're a victim of the ever-present "they." "They" caused the screw-ups. "They" delivered materials late. "They" passed restrictive legislation. "They" didn't provide the needed direction or focus. If a team doesn't get "they" out of its system, it won't be able to learn. Then it will become the "they" that gets in everyone else's way. (And thus is balance preserved.)

Cultures—learning or not—become self-fulfilling prophecies. A company with a conservative culture fills with people who self-select not to take risks and not to admit mistakes. These aren't people who will come rushing with open arms when someone proclaims, "Now we want to start taking risks!"

Shifting a culture means addressing fears with substance: the organization must factor risk-taking into its rewards and performance measures. That support must come out in daily interactions. And even then, the best learning comes from carefully separating judgments from facts, and promoting the search for solutions, rather than rehashing blame. Our society does a great job of squelching learning instincts, but with patience, care, and precise communication, a group can re-create a culture of learning and exploration.

Putting it into action: Run a kick-ass learning review

Focus on the Facts by focusing on the whiteboard. Arrange the group in a semi-circle facing a whiteboard setting up the basic conflict: "us vs. the whiteboard."

Draw out a timeline of the project. Note the major milestones, the major decisions, and any major successes or disasters along the way.

Next, review the timeline and identify what went wrong, without regard to fault. List facts without judgment. If specific people are mentioned, remove the blame and just describe circumstances. "Bob handed in the report late" would become "Report handed in late."

Now make a second list of all the good things that happened. Be specific. "We supported each other" is too vague. "We stayed late and took on each other's work in order to meet a tight deadline" is just about right. At the end of this exercise, this list of specific actions will become a jumping-off point.

For each "bad" event, ask the team:

- What choices *could* we have made to avoid the badness?

- What choices *did* we make that should have been avoided?

- What events, motivations, and actions did we misinterpret that fed into the bad action?

- What were the correct interpretations?
- Given all that, what does this all mean about what we should and shouldn't do going forward?

For each "good" action, ask:

- Was this really because we did something right, or are we taking credit for an act of Nature?
- If it was us, what did we do to cause the goodness?
- Is there anything we didn't do that helped the goodness happen?
- How did our interpretation of events, motivations, and actions help the goodness come to pass?
- Given all that, what does this mean about what we should do and shouldn't do going forward?

Remember: this is about *team* learning. Only bring specific people into the process at the very last questions. If Bob's report was three weeks late, the only question that mentions Bob is the question, "How can the team help Bob get the report done on time?" By discussing facts and framing the team's involvement as one of future joint responsibility, the frame is shifting from "Who did what right/wrong?" to "What happened, and how can we help it happen better next time?"

Chapter 8
Building Your Strategy Using Your Team

"If each of us hires people smaller than we are, we shall become a company of dwarfs."

— David Ogilvy

A CEO had just spent four grueling months on the road fund-raising. He got back to his company, which had grown by about 25% while he was gone, locked himself in his office, and proceeded to redesign the company's strategy assuming he could do it all on his own. He's a smart guy, but he doesn't know how the company operates, what the issues are, and he's overlooked his most valuable resource: the existing executive team.

When you're re-formulating your strategy, use the entire team to build a solid strategy. Rather than trying to direct them, consider your job to be developing the team and letting the team develop the plans. You organize them and point them in the right direction.

---

[1] The material on hedgehog concepts comes from *Good to Great* by Jim Collins. The material on commitments is derived from a talk by Prof. Donald Sull, HBS Professor.

In great teams, each member brings their best to the party. They only do what they're best at, and they do those things superbly. The work gets divided to play to each person's strengths. Your job, should you choose to accept it, is making that happen here and now with your team.

Identify strengths

You can only match work to strengths if you know what strengths people bring to the team! Get everyone together and explore each other's backgrounds, expertise, likes, and dislikes. Match your discoveries to the work, so tasks go to whomever is most likely to finish them well and quickly.

Does a team member have contacts, industry experience, or experience in specific companies that will be valuable to the group? Put them on related tasks. Experience in a functional area or two can make a resident expert in those areas. Those with great people skills should be doing people work, while those who prefer to work behind the scenes can do research and build infrastructure.

Don't limit yourself to obvious business strengths. Mental traits can be even more valuable over time: long-term thinking, short-term thinking, idea orientation, data orientation, comfort with stress, technological comfort, people skills, strategic thinking, ability to challenge assumptions. There are hundreds of ways to slice mental traits, but whatever your framework, know that mental traits become great strengths when matched with the right challenge.

For example, some people prefer to follow established procedures. The business press worships "innovation," "disruption," and "destroying old paradigms." Well, guess what? "Out-of-the-box" disruption is great for occasional big conceptual leaps, but it's the established procedures that drive a successful business. And when boarding a plane, who really wants a disruptive, out-of-the-box pilot, anyway? Give me a pilot who loves completing their sixty-point safety checklist today with the same precision and care they used the first time they went through it.

A strength is nothing more—and nothing less—than a skill so well matched to a task that the results are stellar. Know your team's skills, and you can all begin turning those skills into strengths.

Use your team to hone direction

Once you have the "who" on the team, have them pool resources to choose the "what." You've chosen a business goal, and your team can hone the strategy and tactics you'll use to make it successful. In the book *Good to Great*, Jim Collins suggests that a business choose a single concept—a "hedgehog concept"—as the core of the business strategy. The hedgehog does only one thing: roll into an ironclad ball. But the strategy works so well that it's invincible on its own turf. Your hedgehog concept comes from a brew of your individual values, skills, competencies, and a healthy dose of business sense. The team collectively knows more than any one member, and they'll define the hedgehog concept together.

Passion. Rally around something you can be passionate about. If you're all deeply devoted to children, youngsters, and family, for goodness sake, don't concentrate on publishing HTML reference manuals. Publish books for teens, young adults, and families. Choose a strategy that unleashes your collective inspiration!

Being the best. Your hedgehog concept should be something at which you can be the best in the world. It doesn't mean you *are* the best, just that you can *become* the best. This can be trickier than it seems. Your team members and their skills will contribute to deciding where you can excel. Competition can also affect your choices. Even if you have the perfect team, existing players may have locked up areas of opportunity. If I were starting a discount retail store, for instance, I'd be careful about hedgehog concepts that put me head-to-head with Wal-Mart. "Huge stores with good service" is a concept that's taken. Even a superb team probably couldn't be best in a world dominated by Wal-Mart. But "mom-and-pop style stores with character, suited to blend with local communities" is a niche that is still open[2].

You can divide strengths in many, many ways. Some of the most useful I've found:

Specific "content" strengths:	Generic business strengths:	People strengths:	Mental strengths:
Specific company experience	Functional experience (e.g., finance, marketing, operations)	Management experience	Goal oriented
Experience in the specific business		Ability to motivate others	Fire-fighting oriented
	Operational thinking		Conceptual/Hands-on
Insight into the competition	Marketing thinking	Understanding of how to build culture	Data-driven
			Perfectionist
Market knowledge	Technological understanding	Leadership skills	Pragmatic
Relationships with key suppliers, customers, etc.		Empathy	Action orientation
		Conflict management	Planning orientation
		Negotiating skills	Short-term thinker
			Long-term thinker
			Response to pressure

For a completely different (and extremely valuable) approach to strengths, check out the book **Now, Discover Your Strengths: How to Develop Your Talents and Those of the People You Manage**, by Marcus Buckingham and Donald O. Clifton (Simon & Schuster 2001).

---

[2] Don't go running out to start this on my account. I made up this example. There may be good reasons why this niche doesn't exist.

Economic viability. Your hedgehog concept should make money. You should also be able to identify your economic drivers in the form of a measurable "profit-per-x." Often, the "x" is not obvious. For your strategy to make sense, you may choose a subtle "x." Collins relates the story of a company whose strategy was to cluster stores in one geographic area to be most convenient for customers. Rather than measuring profit per store, the company realized that profit per neighborhood was the key to driving operations, compensation systems, and organizational learning in pursuit of convenience for their customers.

Monitor your team's commitments

As you start implementing, pay close attention to the commitments you make. Commitments provide flexibility and focus, but can bind you to a long-term course of action. You rarely know what the future will bring, so choose commitments wisely. Keep as flexible as possible until you're fairly sure you've chosen the right course.

Commitments come in all shapes and sizes, but some of the most powerful are the agreements you make on how to frame the world. Your beliefs about what customers want and how they behave, if propagated throughout your company, are a very powerful frame. Ken Olsen, founder of Digital Equipment Corporation, was famous for rejecting IBM's frame that computers meant room-sized boxes that were only useful to large corporations. He built DEC and revolutionized the industry by inventing the minicomputer. Unfortunately, he got caught in his frame of the minicomputer being The Answer. Oops. In the late 1990s, his once leading-company was acquired by upstart PC maker Compaq.

Supplier and distributor relationships can become commitments. Decisions to vertically integrate (or not) can become commitments. Deeply held cultural values can become commitments. Large capital expenditures can become commitments. One entrepreneur recently told me his company had perfected the ability to open a new market and quickly achieve a 25%-plus profit margin. Unfortunately, while going up their learning curve, they built facilities several times their optimal size. The company's survival is still touch-and-go—not because it's a bad business, but because early commitments have saddled the company with unproductive, expensive assets.

Become a leader, not a manager

Finally, spend your own time leading rather than managing. You've got a good team, and you've jointly chosen a direction. Now your job is keeping the company on track. Keep your team working well together, and make sure you're building a company where everyone plays to their strengths. Know your hedgehog concept, discuss it regularly, and make sure it guides the company's daily decisions. Spend time thinking strategically with your management team. Have them project the hedgehog concept out one, three, or five years into the future, and steer the company and its commitments toward that reality.

Your job is creating an environment where *your team* can do their best. Give them all the credit. Recognize and celebrate their accomplishments. When they screw up, lead an "after-action review" to help them learn. Remember that you're building a culture that brings out and amplifies everyone's *strengths*, so use mistakes as an opportunity to reexamine the strengths of the team and change your tactics, your assumptions, or your organization. You have the crew; together you've charted the course. Now stand back and let them bring the dream to fruition.

Chapter 9
Motivating When Times are Tough

"In motivating people, you've got to engage their minds and their hearts. I motivate people, I hope, by example—and perhaps by excitement, by having productive ideas to make others feel involved."

— Keith Rupert Murdoch

It's funny, being a human being. You would think that when the pressure is on, we would flip into resourceful, productive mindsets and valiantly overcome whatever obstacles block the path to our goals. Alas, it doesn't happen that way. When we feel scared and uncertain, our forebrain shuts down and our hindbrain screams, "Run!" That worked great when spotting the saber-tooth tiger grinning at us through the grass. But in the modern world, it's often the opposite of what we need for survival.

Fear motivates immediacy

Creating urgency is a first step in mobilizing organizations. But an important truth about humans is that urgency easily slips into fear. Fear mobilizes, and

> **"** Fear motivates people strongly,
> but in random directions. Leadership
> aligns them in the same direction. **"**

it mobilizes *away from the perceived danger.* Which way is "away from?" Whichever direction someone is pointed when that hindbrain screams "Run!" Everyone around will also move quickly—in whatever direction they happen to be facing. Fear gets people moving *now,* but it won't move them in the same direction.

Fear does more harm than just scatter effort; it produces stress. Under stress, creativity vanishes, problem-solving abilities diminish, and people stop learning. They react from impulse, they don't think through consequences of their actions, and they become less able to spot patterns and interconnections. This is fine for a five-minute burst of jungle adrenaline, but it won't lead to a workforce that can navigate a tricky economy.

Any workforce living in stress will have problems over the long term. When morale is bad for months at a time, people disengage. They stop thinking about taking the company to new heights and start groaning when the alarm clock goes off—and groans just don't bring out peak performance.

Leadership motivates coordinated action

Fear's companion is, oddly, leadership. Fear motivates people strongly, but in random directions. Leadership aligns them in the same direction. Call it what you will: inspiration, vision, mission—setting direction gives people something to *move toward.* By sharing a vision, everyone in an organization can orient themselves around the same set of high-level goals.

Working toward a larger purpose also mobilizes people, but it mobilizes them in a way that unlocks their creativity, problem-solving, and resourceful mental states. When working toward a large goal they perceive as achievable but challenging, people create *eustress*, a positive stress that gives them the energy and resources to make progress on the goal.

It's a big improvement when everyone is moving in the same direction, but one more piece is needed: coordination. The balance between good stress and bad stress is delicate. Once people agree on a goal and are psyched to go there, coordination becomes even more important. If two groups become blocked by a lack of coordination, bad stress can re-emerge and begin shutting down morale again. So once people are mobilized, the ongoing challenge is making sure they're supporting each other, and not getting in each other's way.

Reconnect leadership at the top

The first step to getting a workforce into a powerful, productive mental state is to start with you. You've probably got the "Run!" response down cold. Now it's time to reconnect with your "toward" vision. People take emotional cues from their leaders, and if you've been stressed about the economy, you'll be radiating it throughout your organization, so get yourself and your leadership team into a powerful, positive place.

> **"** Have your teams ask continually,
> 'Will this decision move us further in
> the direction we wish to go?' **"**

Leave the daily triggers that pull you back into stress. Turn on the voicemail, turn off the e-mail, smash the cell phone, and head off for a weekend in a mountain cabin. Get enough sleep, enough food, and enough physical relaxation so your brain starts working again. Reconnect to your vision. Write, daydream, and brainstorm where you want your group in five years, a year, six months, and three months. Factor in your personal goals as well so you really tap your own intrinsic motivation.

You'll know you've done enough when you feel a strong pull toward your goals. Uncertainties may still lurk in the background, but once you've regained your equilibrium, you will also feel a strong sense of where you're going.

Spread that feeling to the rest of your leadership team. Invite them for an off-site, and together, clarify the vision of where you're headed until it's at least as clear as perceptions about current problems. Take the time to make sure everyone understands the direction. Bring in their goals, wishes, and aspirations for the organization. While you work, watch their faces. Notice the energy level. When they start getting excited, you've tapped their motivation and gotten them back on a powerful path.

Back to the business, decrease stress

Once you return to daily business, you'll have to decrease stress as you align people. Stress from specific causes ("My kids are sick") can be addressed on an ad hoc basis. Stress from vague sources like "the economy" is general anxiety. Often, you can help people by just letting them talk. Listen empathetically and don't rush into solving or analyzing problems (for most of us type-As, this is much, much harder than it sounds). Feeling listened-to can be enough to help someone regain equilibrium.

If the anxiety is about Things We Don't Really Like to Talk About—like the fear of layoffs—talking can help defuse them. There's no better way to nurture a fear than to let it remain the stuff of speculation. When left to their imaginations, people deal with uncertainty by imagining the worst and then reacting as if it had already happened. Truth is a great antidote for uncertainty. It is, after all, a form of certainty. Discuss what's happening, even if all you can say is, "No one knows what will happen, but we'll keep forging ahead toward our goals."

Oh, yes. Keeping people healthy is also essential to soothing their nerves. Make sure people are sleeping enough. Research is showing that even a little lost sleep means major lost productivity and creativity while awake. Sixteen-hour work days are probably as productive as ten-hour days with sleep and an after-work life.

Connect people to forward motivation

As you decrease stress, have the leadership team bring the sense of direction into all interactions. Remind people about the direction. Rally them. Excite them. But don't overdo it; this isn't about creating a huge one-time pep rally high. You're setting a direction for the organization that you want to pervade decision-making and keep people steady over the long term.

You build the strongest connections when decisions are made. Have your teams ask continually, "Will this decision move us further in the direction we wish to go?" Once everyone unifies around this question, coordination becomes possible and it will be much easier for people to move forward, which is what productivity is all about.

Your job becomes keeping your leadership team tied to the company vision, and helping them propagate the vision to their teams in turn. People are more productive when they know where they're going and feel like they stand a chance of getting there. By reducing their stress and fear, addressing their uncertainty, and linking everyday activities to a future direction, people will be able to concentrate on producing results, rather than just running in circles from their anxiety's imaginary monsters.

Chapter 10
Time Spent Fund-Raising Can Be Deadly

"Money is of no value; it cannot spend itself. All depends on the skill of the spender."

— *Ralph Waldo Emerson*

"I just hit a major home run!" exclaimed the entrepreneur.

"Did you ship product? Did you make your first sale? Did you get a large contract?" asked his friend.

"No, no. Something much better: today we closed on a $20 million round of financing."

Small businesses are always strapped for cash. Even large businesses, when growing, are strapped for cash. As part of a company's leadership team, it's easy to get caught up in fund-raising-related activities. When you raise a round of financing, congratulate yourself for raising money, but don't think it was time well spent. You need money to stay in business, but raising it destroys value: money changes hands, with a big chunk siphoning off to lawyers, filing fees, travel expenses, and phone calls. You're left with less than when you started, and that's before buying your first paper clip! Money may make the business *viable*, but it doesn't make it valuable.

Nor does fund-raising use your time wisely. Investors and banks are betting on what your team uniquely brings to the table. Your competitors have all raised money, too. That's nothing special. Fund-raising ability doesn't distinguish you one whit. What does distinguish you is time spent bringing your vision to life by building your organization.

Actually, investors would love it if you never raised money again! Every new share of stock issued dilutes current shareholders. With every dollar you raise, existing investors wince. In the late 1990s, many companies raised so much capital that they would have needed to be in the Fortune 10 to give investors a decent return. 10,000 companies can't *all* be in the Fortune 10. And as we saw, none of them made it.

> **" Money may make the business viable,
> but it doesn't make it valueable "**

And beware! Successful fund-raising can snare the executives involved! It lets them avoid their real challenge—building a stellar business—in favor of the "success" of a $20 million closing. You see, fund-raising is time-consuming, but really rather easy: the customers are venture capitalists, private equity firms, angel investors, and banks. Their buying criteria is simple and public—most of them will even outline it on their web site. And the products, your business plan and sales pitch, can be created by one or two people.

Running a company is much more challenging. You don't necessarily know your customers. In fact, you may find they don't even exist! If you do have customers, you may not know their buying criteria. In fact, *they* may not know their buying criteria! And delivering your product and services means coordinating dozens of people, each with different priorities and demands on their time. Yet knowing the customer and delivering the product will make or break you. Fund-raising is a stressful—but much safer—place for an entrepreneur to spend their time.

So yeah, someone has to raise money. Businesses need money to operate. If you aren't yet profitable, that means pitching investors, haggling over terms, and re-pricing your round at the 13th hour. Just remember that getting the money merely opens the starting gate. Then it's time to add value, and you add far more value as a leader and manager than you do as a fund-raiser. So raise your money, then run your business. Run it well and profitably and you'll repay your investors a dozen times over.

Chapter 11
Measuring a CEO's Success

"An inflated consciousness is always egocentric and conscious of nothing but its own existence. It is incapable of learning from the past, incapable of understanding contemporary events, and incapable of drawing right conclusions about the future. It is hypnotized by itself and therefore cannot be argued with. It inevitably dooms itself to calamities that must strike it dead."

— Carl Jung

The higher up you are in an organization, the more global your job. The more global your job, the harder it is to define success. The CEO is the biggest job, the hardest to define, yet one where measuring success is most critical.

Unlike inconvenient lower-level jobs, *no one tells the Chief Executive how she's doing.* Do managers let her know she's undermining their authority, making poor decisions, or communicating poorly? Not likely. Even when a CEO asks for honest feedback, the fear is there, that non-flattering feedback may stall a promising career. Even when a company uses 360-degree feedback, no one penalizes the CEO if she doesn't act on the feedback.

The Board of Directors supposedly oversees the CEO, but they are far removed from day-to-day actions. Over time, they can evaluate performance, but they look mainly at share price and company strategy. They are rarely interested in—(or qualified to comment on)—the CEO's daily behavior.

But the CEO's daily behavior will make or break the company! The CEO's duties don't change because they are unmeasured. Indeed, lax measurement makes it easy for the CEO to feel confident, even when she shouldn't. Good feedback is the only way to know what's working, but share price doesn't do it. External measures measure the company, not the link to the CEO's actions. A low share price tells her something's wrong, but it doesn't help her figure out what.

By measuring her performance based on her duties, a CEO can learn to do her job better. The CEO's job is setting strategy and vision, building culture, leading the senior team, and allocating capital. The last of these is easy to measure. The first three are more of a challenge.

How does a CEO know she's doing the vision thing? It's hard. *Having* vision isn't enough—that just takes a handful of mushrooms and a vision quest. *Communicating* vision is the key. When people "get it," they know how their daily job supports the vision. If they can't link their job to the vision, that tells a CEO that her communication is faulty, or she hasn't helped her managers turn the vision into actual tasks. Either way, a CEO can monitor her success as a visionary by questioning and listening for employees to link their jobs with the company vision.

Culture building is subtle. The culture a CEO sees may be very different from the culture of the rank-and-file. One company had a facilities policy that all equipment within 450 feet of the senior management offices was kept in top working order. Senior managers saw a smoothly running company, while everyone else saw neglect and carelessness.

Surveys about openness, values, and morale can be used to develop a measure of culture. The questions to ask aren't rocket science. The book *First, Break all the Rules* gives a great questionnaire for measuring overall culture. Also, check turnover. When 95% of your workforce says they can't wait to get to work, something is going right. If people rarely leave and it's easy to attract top talent at below-market prices, you can be sure the culture plays a large role. If people leave (especially your top performers), again—look to culture. And don't underestimate the power of walking around and counting smiles. If people are having fun, it will show.

The CEO's success at team-building can often be measured through the team. Teams know when they're effective. They can also rate their team using assessments that measure specific behaviors. For example, "I can trust my teammates." "My teammates deliver their part of the project on time." "Every member knows what is expected of them." Regular team self-assessments can help the CEO track the team's progress and hone her abilities to keep the team running smoothly.

Easiest to measure is a CEO's capital allocation skill. In fact, financial measures are the ones made public: earnings and share price. But how can a CEO link those to her actual decisions? Working with her CFO, a CEO can devise financial measures appropriate to her business. Sometimes traditional measures are most appropriate, such as economic value added or return on assets (for a capital-intensive company). Other times, the CEO may want to invent business-specific measures, such as return on training dollars, for a company which values state-of-the-art training for employees. By monitoring several such measures, a CEO learns to link her budget decisions with company outcomes. Ultimately, the CEOs should be creating more than a dollar of value for every dollar invested in the company. Otherwise, her best bet is to return cash to the shareholders for them to invest in more productive vehicles.

In startups, earnings begin low to nonexistent, and share price is more about salesmanship and vision than earnings. So the CEO gets almost no useful feedback about her capital allocation wisdom. She doesn't know whether a dollar spent on a slightly nicer-than-necessary copy machine is wasted or is a wise investment in the long-term. Careful attention to the design and tracking of financial measures can help her prepare for the transition to an earnings-driven company.

Chapter 12
When Power Goes to Your Head

*"However big the fool, there is
always a bigger fool to admire him."*

— Nicolas Boileau-Despréau

A top manager can tank a company by not knowing what they're doing, misunderstanding their duties, or failing to set up good measurement systems. But the job can fight back and screw the person even more. It's said that power corrupts, and what's more powerful than being top management? We may love political democracies, but our companies are legal dictatorships. It may be great fun playing Boss, but it may take a very human toll.

It's all too easy for a top manager to become a ... jerk ... without realizing it. They can forget—if they ever knew—what it was like to have a boss. News they don't want to hear? Ignored. Negative feedback? Never happened. And no one will call them to task for it. They can bypass the chain of command beneath them and meddle to their heart's content. Their income becomes less and less linked to their daily actions, and they can rake in boatloads of money, genuinely believing they deserve it. Most dreadfully, they can forget what it is like to be "one of the little people." I was present for this conversation:

Worker	I have to leave early today.
VP	Why?
Worker	To pick up my kids from daycare.
VP	Oh... (*genuinely perplexed*) ... Why don't you have your nanny do that?
Worker	I don't have a nanny.
VP	Oh... (*wanders away with a mildly confused expression*)

The worker was an incredibly productive person. She worked harder than the VP had ever worked, got more done, yet couldn't have afforded a nanny if her life depended on it. The VP didn't intend to be a jerk, but his lack of empathy didn't win many supporters.

Arrogance comes from externalizing blame

Having little day-to-day accountability can also turn a top boss sour. When things go wrong, she can blame everyone around her without facing her own shortcomings. "My employees just don't get it," laments an executive, never thinking for a moment that *she* is the one who hired them. Did she hire incompetents? Or has she failed to communicate goals consistently and clearly? "Market conditions have changed," she declares. A nice excuse, but isn't it top management's job to anticipate the market and position the company for success under a variety of scenarios? Without someone to keep her honest, she can gradually absolve herself of all responsibility.

Believing a title can lead to overconfidence

Arrogance also threatens top managers. "Because I have this great title, I must know the business better than anyone else." Uh huh. It could be the Peter Principle in effect—someone has reached their level of incompetence. No one can be an expert in all functional areas. An executive's job is spending time with the big picture. If she knows the details better than her employees, she's either hiring the wrong people or spending her time at the wrong levels of the organization. It's appropriate to manage operations if absolutely necessary, but she should quickly hire good operational managers and return to leading her organization.

Sometimes, an exec can come to believe their title grants infallibility. Watch out for those! Even the Pope is only infallible a couple of times each century. But higher salaries (surely she deserves it! After all, salary benchmarks show how underpaid she is) and great perks reinforce delusions of grandeur. Then when layoffs come, the executive wants applause for having the moral strength to make "hard choices," quietly overlooking how her own poor decision making led to the need for layoffs.

Top positions can hurt learning

Of course, once infallible, there's nothing more to learn, and top managers may quietly stop learning. Without daily oversight and high quality feedback on how they do their job, they can mistakenly believe their actions lead to success. In reality, they may be doing the wrong things, but a great staff may be working around the clock to cover the mistakes.

Furthermore, sins of omission aren't penalized. An executive who does an adequate job, but far less than she could/should have done—goes unnoticed. In hindsight, Acme Software could have had a $1 billion market niche, and gone public with a valuation of tens of billions. Instead, it stuck to one product, had little understanding of its markets, and ignored competition. Yet it still went public in a $300-million IPO. Was management penalized for a lack of vision and market responsiveness? Hardly! The top managers walked off with $60 million apiece, reinforcing the notion that they had done a great job. Yet with a slightly grander vision, the company might have been 10 or 100 times its size. (At least one top manager, believing himself a strategic genius, has since tanked a number of companies foolish enough to listen to his advice.)

Setting vision is the job of top managers, but there's no one to raise a fuss if the sights are too low. There's no penalty for missing the grander vision. Such sins of omission are an executive's worst enemy. She can be lulled into mediocrity by not knowing what would have been possible. The four-minute mile was considered impossible... until Roger Bannister ran it. Now, it's commonplace.

Though salary benchmarks are common, performance benchmarks are surprisingly rare. Quality learning demands an executive benchmark herself against other superb execs. Her central learning question is not "are you doing a good job?" but "could I be doing a better job and if so, how can I learn to measure up?"

Chapter 13
Action Plan for Keeping a Cool Head When You've Got the Power

"The worst disease which can afflict executives in their work is not, as popularly supposed, alcoholism; it's egotism."

— Harold S. Geneen

This action plan will help you avoid some of the pitfalls of having a top job. The steps are simple, easy, and you can do them quickly. They'll help you stay connected with workers, keep yourself humble, and learn while becoming more successful. The suggestions strive to be quick and easy to do, while still producing real results.

Make space to practice these assignments

Set aside 15 minutes daily to developing as a leader and human being. This will be the time you think about the below topics and set your mind for the day. Schedule the time if necessary. Just make sure that you do what's right for your growth. Your first instinct will be to think that you can't possibly set aside this much time. Sure you can. It's only 15 minutes, but you have to make the commitment.

Pace yourself. Life is long. Adopt these suggestions one or two at a time, and practice until you make them your own. Then move on. Forcing won't help; this is about developing at your own natural rhythm. Do one assignment for a few weeks, then move on to another. Keep the ones that work for you and drop those that don't.

Staying connected with "the little people"

Cultivate an attitude of respect—your respect for them. The "little people" are the ones making your goals into reality. Meditate on this for a few minutes and ask yourself whether you can do their jobs as well as they can. If you can, then you're not hiring the right people—go change that! Otherwise, once a day, go talk to one of your low-level employees—someone more capable than you in their area of expertise—and learn from them. Choose a different person each day. Get as close to the front line workers as possible.

Listen with an open mind and learn. Learn about their job. Ask what works for them and what doesn't. Above all, listen to their comments without judgment. Your goal is to connect with their experience of the world, not impose your own. Learn about their lives. Find out what motivates them. Why are they working for you instead of someone else? Simply by spending a few minutes understanding their lives, you can greatly increase your appreciation of how they're different (and similar!).

Share your vision and job with them from a position of service. Pretend that your job is to make this person a success at making the company a success. Ask them how their job fits into the work the company does. If they don't know, take on the responsibility of helping them understand how their job links to the vision. Clarify any confusion they may have about where the company is going. And ask them what you can do to help them succeed at doing their best. Then do it.

Staying humble

Acknowledge, often! Without your employees, your dreams and plans wouldn't amount to much. Take every available opportunity to acknowledge the contribution of those around you and give them credit, especially in public. Feedback is rare in most companies, and positive feedback is rarest of all. When in doubt, give them the credit and you take all the blame. If you're worried about your reputation, don't be. As your teams deliver ongoing stellar results, people will figure out you made a contribution.

"Get" that it's all your responsibility. When things don't go the way you want, take responsibility—whether or not it's your fault. The mindset of responsibility will put you in a much more powerful place than the mindset of blame. Regularly review circumstances asking, "What could I do differently (or stop doing) to make a positive difference?" Identify the action and then take it. You'll be surprised how much more power you have over externalities, operating from responsibility rather than blame.

Gather honest advisors to hold you accountable for your behavior. You probably have outcome measurements already. Make sure you get feedback on how you do your day-to-day job. Actively solicit feedback from third parties: friends, peers, and associates. Share your issues and how you're handling them, and ask for an honest assessment. Make yourself accountable as best you can.

Identify your limits. Ask "Can someone else in the world do my job better than I am currently doing it?" If the answer is Yes, seek out that person and ask for their guidance in getting better. If the answer is No, validate

71

that answer by asking your advisors, competitors, suppliers, customers, and employees. Many companies have crashed and burned because they believed they were the best, for no good reason but pride and ego.

Create measurable performance criteria for your team, including yourself. Make sure people know their goals, and know what they can count on you to deliver in helping them reach those goals. Hold yourselves accountable. If you don't meet your goals, refuse your bonus, take no raise, and treat yourself exactly as you would treat an employee who missed their targets. It sends a powerful message to the company you're serious about performance.

Ask your direct reports, your boss or your Board, and anyone else you work with for feedback a couple of times a year. You can use a 360-degree feedback process or simply ask in an e-mail. It's a lot easier to hear feedback on your performance if you've explicitly asked for it.

Videotape yourself receiving bad news. Watch the videotape and decide whether or not you would want to work for that person. If the answer is No, learn to chill when you hear bad news.

Learning well

Study excellent leaders. Call a leader you admire and invite them to lunch. Exchange tips and adopt tactics that others have found useful. Read books like *First, Break All the Rules*, which are broad-based studies of habits of top-performers. Adopt at least one new habit a month.

Create systems for gathering feedback. Interview customers, competitors, analysts, and others in your industry to know how your company and products are perceived. Make sure you're gathering feedback that will disconfirm your belief about the world, as much as confirm it. For example, if you think you're #1 in your market, don't just ask customers why they like your products. Ask what other products they use, and how your products fall short.

Spend time learning about the fundamentals of a top executive job:

- Setting and sharing strategy. The strategy and vision for the company determine where everyone will focus their efforts. Find a vision and strategy and use it to align your entire company.

- Advancing the corporate culture. Your culture will determine what people do and don't try, who will stay, who will leave, and how business will get done. Culture starts with you. Decide how you want people to act and start modeling the behavior publicly.

- Making sure resources are spent wisely. Part of your job is using the company's resources as prudently as possible. Every dollar you spend should produce more than $1 of return for the company, or it's a waste of money. Learn how to make these judgments.

- Hiring and Firing. A major part of your job is team and culture building. Hiring and firing are must-have skills. Read, take classes, and review past hiring successes and mistakes. Do whatever you can to hone your abilities.

Raise the bar

Hold yourself to higher standards next year than you did this year. Challenge yourself to learn to get more done with fewer hours and fewer resources while creating a more balanced life for yourself.

These are just a few of the things you can do to increase your chances for success as a senior executive. A coach can also help you identify and overcome (or compensate for) blocks in your performance. Success can be had with many different skill sets. The more you learn about yourself and your capabilities, the better you will be able to shape a job that works for you. The more you learn about the capabilities of those around you, the better you will be able to build teams that produce spectacular results.

Part 2

Leading with Vision— Getting Things Done through Other People

"Three 'ayes', two 'nays' and one who's 'jiggy' with it."

Chapter 14
The Essence of Leadership

"Becoming a leader is synonymous with becoming yourself. It is precisely that simple, and it is also that difficult."

— Warren Bennis

My coaching clients' number one complaint? "There's no leadership at this company." I hear it across industries, in companies of all sizes. But what *is* business leadership? We often confuse "business leadership" with "someone with a CEO title who made the Forbes 400 list when their company did well." Yet when people say their company needs leadership, impressive job titles and large salaries just aren't what's missing.

We say, "So-and-so is a born leader." No such thing. Leadership is a *relationship* between a person and a group. *Successful* leadership adds in the skill of guiding a group to success. In any relationship, success depends on both parties. One group's stellar leader may fail utterly when leading another group.

Rather than just study leaders (11,000 books on leadership cover that ground), you can learn a lot by asking people who they follow and why. They will tell you that leadership is emotional; it's about inspiration, motivation, and connection. Unlike management, it doesn't lend itself to systems, structure, and traditional classroom teaching. What inspires people to follow is surprisingly consistent, and surprisingly simple. But be forewarned: Simple doesn't mean easy!

Establishing the leadership relationship

Call it "vision," "mission," or "shared delusion," but it all boils down to one thing: First and foremost, people look to leaders for *direction*. Only by knowing their organization's direction can people apply themselves to achieve their goals. It needn't be formally stated; the leader's actions and decisions convey the direction to the company. The direction needs to pervade every decision and conversation within the company, and it's the leader who makes that happen. Providing direction for others is a key to creating a leadership relationship.

> **"** First and foremost, people look to leaders for direction. **"**

Even with direction, people must *trust* a leader. Trust is built on honesty and integrity. People want the truth from their leaders. Outrage from Watergate, the Monica Lewinsky affair, Enron, and many other public scandals were fueled less by the events than by the accused parties' cover-ups and lies. When Salomon Brothers covered up improper trading in an early-1990s scandal, it fueled the flight of a billion-dollars' worth of customers as people lost trust in the organization. Warren Buffett rescued the company by using complete and total candor with Wall Street and regulators as a way of restoring trust. Far from being a disaster, telling the truth proved astonishingly effective in quickly restoring the company's integrity with a minimum of fines.

Leaders must have *integrity,* establishing clear values and living those values. One of my clients worked for a newly public company whose CEO urged employees to hold their shares to keep investor confidence high. He then sold several million-dollars' worth of his own shares. He responded to his employees' feelings of betrayal saying, "It was just a small percentage of my holdings." But that didn't matter! He contradicted himself by selling shares while exhorting his employees to hold theirs. It killed his leadership.

Interestingly, the key is having actions match values, more so than what those values are. If one leader values quality and another values speed-to-market, they will simply attract different people to their organizations. But in either case, they must live their values consistently.

Consistency is another vital leadership element. When a leader changes direction with the market fad-of-the-day, or when his or her values shift according to the latest public opinion polls, people stop following. People want dependable leaders who provide a touchstone in times of change. You may ask: In a world of constant change, don't we need to shift and adapt? Of course. But you must choose a direction and values that stay stable even while adapting your tactics.

A software company once had a company vision, "We will produce the best ABC widget for DOS the world has every seen." It was a great vision statement, until Windows squashed the company out of existence. The software maker's vision was so narrow it couldn't adapt to change. A mission of, "We will solve the ABC problem for computers worldwide" would have been flexible enough to keep the vision while adapting to technological evolution.

" Vision, integrity, consistency, and connection create the leadership relationship. "

Lastly, followers need to feel *connected* to their leaders. Leaders almost always connect through shared values; that's one reason followers leave when a leader doesn't live his or her values. Helping people feel they are part of something much greater—giving them a personal vision—is another strong tactic. For instance, a leader in the healthcare industry may say, "You're not just joining our company, you're becoming part of transforming the world of healthcare." Recognizing and rewarding employee achievement helps cement the connection. On the other hand, taking credit for others' work is a powerful connection destroyer.

I was surprised by this framework's simplicity—direction, integrity, consistency, and connection. But its simplicity hides how difficult it is to pull off. It's difficult because these qualities can't be faked for long. Creating a direction is easy. Integrating it into every breath and decision is not. Choosing values is easy. Aligning behavior, decision-making, policies, and organization around those values is not. Consistency is easy … until things don't go quite as planned. And connection is easy until things get busy and instinct tells us to stop all this fluffy foolishness and just get down to work.

Building the organization

Direction, integrity, consistency, and connection create the leadership relationship. That's a first step in building an organization, but it doesn't address the issue of how leaders make their organizations successful. History is littered with great leaders who didn't have a clue how to turn their leadership into an enduring business. Let me share some of the highlights:

- Focus, focus, focus. Know what the organization should be doing and ruthlessly say "no" to anything that would be a distraction.

- Play to individual strengths. Understand the abilities of everyone you hire and make sure their job plays to their strengths. Don't spend too much time developing weak areas. If someone can go from good-to-great in their strength, that's more valuable to the organization than taking someone from poor-to-acceptable. Build organizational competence by teaming up complementary skill sets. Ditto for yourself; know what you're good at and can do well, and spend most of your time doing that.

- Play to organizational strengths. Stick to what you're good at as a company, and get very good at it. If you're a great software company, opening a chain of high-end fashion clothing stores won't build a strong organization.

- You can train people for skills, but it's *much* harder to train attitude. Most companies hire for specific job history or resume keywords, which is precisely the wrong way to go about it. Hire for attitude first.

- Bring out the best in your people. Hire the best, give them a common direction, and let them do their job. You'll have a much stronger organization than if you make yourself too important. Remember: Every time you hire someone who isn't as smart as you, you lower the average IQ of the company.

You'll notice that I've defined leadership as mostly "soft" skills. It is. When it comes to leadership, I remember what the Vice-Chairman of a multibillion-dollar company once told me: "At the end of the day the financial and strategic issues are there but they are reducible largely by analytics... the people and process issues are not." If your goal is to become a successful business leader, your route will be smoother if you spend some time working on relationship skills and "softer" aspects of leading. Because at its heart, leadership is nothing more and nothing less than inspiring others to follow your dream and doing what it takes to make possible their success.

Chapter 15
Leadership Begins with a Strong Vision
You Can't Lead if You Don't Know Where You're Going

"Good business leaders create a vision, articulate the vision, passionately own the vision, and relentlessly drive it to completion."

— Jack Welch

Martin Luther King Jr. was one of the most prominent and revered leaders of the Civil Rights movement in the sixties in America. He spoke passionately about his vision of a country in which white and black people could live side-by-side, without skin color blinding us to each other's value. His most famous speech is "I have a Dream," which painted his vision clearly and forcefully. To this day, it remains one of the most inspiring speeches I've ever read.

Dr. King's leadership was partially based on his personal charisma and inspiration, which he used to forge a vision that has long outlived him. This "visionary" style of leadership is very powerful; it gives people a powerful sense of direction along with an idea of what to expect once they arrive. Creating and conveying a vision relies on passion. If a vision doesn't engage people emotionally, it won't be a powerful motivator.

A vision portrays where you're going. It offers a world—different from the here and now—where people want to live, badly enough to take bold steps to get there. Building a vision for your organization is important, and you begin by building a vision for yourself.

Base your vision on passion

What do you care about so passionately that you would overcome any obstacle to get there? Think about the times you've argued with someone until you were blue in the face, refusing to let yourself be swayed by logic, illogic, or emotion, because you believed so strongly. You were tapping into your power, and that's the power that will help you create a vision to keep you going.

Think back over those times and ask yourself what principles were driving you. Did you care about changing the world? About making sure everyone got fed? About raising your children in a way you believe will give them the best chances for success?

Be honest with yourself as to the source of the passion. If you're thinking of times you were passionate just because you wanted to be right, lay those times aside and find other examples. You're searching for the underlying values that drive you. Make note of the principles that involve other people:

- A dream of taking Humankind to the stars.

- A wish to help others master their fears of hang-gliding.

- A passion to be remembered as having improved people's lives.

- A desire to build a community and connection.

Be honest; if it isn't passion, but just anger or frustration or the desire to be right, keep searching. You want a passion that involves somehow changing the world around you.

Create a vision

Thinking about your passion, ask how the world would be different if your passion were realized. The richer the vision inside your head, the more it will come through when you're in a leadership role.

How would the world be different? What is the visible impact of your vision? It may be small—your living room might be painted a different color. Or it could be huge. Times Square in New York City used to be a seedy red-light district. Someone at Disney had a vision of the square as an attractive, entertaining family destination. And it came to pass!

Who would be touched by your passion? How would they be different? Orrin Hudson founded BeSomeOne.org with the vision of helping disadvantaged kids turn their lives around and succeed in the world.

What would be the concerns of the day? If your passion is to build a manned space station, you might envision a world where the daily news reports on the progress of the station, with people eagerly awaiting the next milestone.

The richer your creation, the more you and your organization will be able to use it for guidance. If you spend the time to flesh out your vision, you can use it to anticipate the alliances you'll need to build, the obstacles you're likely to face, and the capabilities you must develop.

Don't bother limiting yourself to what you think is realistic or doable. A vision isn't about reality. It's about possibility. It's about inspiration and setting direction, not making specific plans. Dream big! If you shoot for the moon, you might only make it to the top of Mt. Everest, but hey, you made it to the top of Everest!

Communicate your vision

Once you have your vision, communicate it. Let people know. Since it's rooted in emotion, you'll automatically present it with intensity. Let the passion drive your presentation, but keep it calm. Direct the passion into inspiration, debate, and discussion—not argument.

You can hook your listeners by engaging them in deepening the vision. Just saying, "Here's my vision" isn't enough. You need others to adopt it as *their* vision, too. So ask them questions that make them engage. If you're sharing your dream of inner city schools, ask "How do *you* think we would choose our teachers once we have our schools set up?" When other people start problem solving around your vision, they'll take ownership of it as well.

Be prepared for doubters. No matter how passionate you are, some people won't be inspired by your vision. That's okay. Plenty of people weren't inspired by Martin Luther King's vision, either. Being a leader isn't about persuading the world, it's about building your corner of the world. Use your vision as a tool for attracting people who *are* inspired and want to join you in making the dream real.

Chapter 16
Creating Your Identity as a Leader: Authority is Not Enough

"The first responsibility of a leader is to define reality. The last is to say thank you. In between, the leader is a servant."

— Max Depree

Eric was about to scream. His latest plan somehow wasn't moving forward. Once again, his employees left the planning meeting and went right back to what they were doing, as if his presentation hadn't even happened. Eric didn't realize that being "the boss" didn't make him a leader. You can be a good executive by mastering the job requirements, but that's management, not leadership. Leading people is not so clear cut. Leadership isn't a job; it's a relationship. Without followers, you can't lead. But you won't be able to lead others until you can lead yourself! Begin your growth as a leader by creating an identity of leadership.

Leave your follower mentality behind

The first step is deceptively simple: choose. You probably said "Yes" to your job as a conscious decision. Now decide you will begin leading. My friend Marla was running a research consortium with a board of six CEOs. She was looking to them for direction, while they were looking to her. One finally took her aside. "Marla, there is no CEO-initiation ceremony. You just need to step up and do it." It is a simple, but necessary mental shift. Step up and do it.

Do it by accepting responsibility to make things happen. Lots of things in his company bugged Mark. Marketing promised deliverables that operations couldn't meet. His boss was abrasive. The lunchroom coffee was too cold. And poor Mark had to get his job done in spite of all these obstacles. He was a victim of a bad situation. But it was his decision to be the victim.

Mark's big shift was deciding he would create his future, rather than respond to it, even if he didn't have the formal authority to affect all the pieces. Mark identified each problem's key players, educated them about the situation, and championed finding and implementing a solution. But nothing would have happened if Mark hadn't decided that he had the power to change his world.

At the executive level, the concerns are different, but the principle is the same. If things aren't going the way you want, take it on yourself to change them. Of course, there are limits to your time and budget, so you'll have to pick and choose your battles, but the attitude you want to adopt is one of being the initiator, builder, and solver of problems.

Think people, not problems

Management is about tools and process. Leadership is about people. Start thinking about the "who" rather than the "what." Mark didn't have the authority to change everything he wanted changed, so he asked himself who he could rally to his cause. He began persuading and cajoling until he was able to get everyone around him to help create the work environment he wanted. Rather than concentrating on how to fix the problems, he convinced others that the problems needed fixing and then encouraged *them* to do the fixing. Leading is all about getting things done through other people.

"Getting things done" means setting a direction. Choose your direction and start going. Make your goals clear to those around you, and use every opportunity to help people understand how their actions are bringing you closer or farther from the goal.

"Through other people" means inspiring others to join in your quest. Some people will buy into the direction—they become the community you're leading. Others won't. That's fine; they can wait outside. You want to attract the people who share your vision, and you need to let others go their own way. Your people skills can make or break you here. If someone needs to go their own way, you want them leaving on an upbeat note.

Leadership is seduction

Managers push, leaders pull. Managers use punishments and rewards, structure, process, deadlines, and milestones to get things done. And it all works, but it isn't leadership. As a leader, think of yourself differently: you seduce. You tantalize with a vision of how the world could be... but only if people are willing and able to rise to the challenge. You motivate and energize. And while management skills (yours or others') may be necessary to get the job done, your identity remains one of inspiration and guidance.

Putting it into action:

- Adopt an attitude of making things happen. Identify three complaints you have about your home or work that you wish somebody else would take care of. Then be the somebody. Take charge, make it happen.

- Identify a problem you're trying to solve, or a goal you're trying to reach. Now ask yourself, "If I couldn't work on this goal myself, but had to get it done through other people, who would I choose? How would I motivate them to *want* to solve the problem?"

- Change from a push to a pull approach. Take a task or project you're currently using punishments and rewards to motivate, and spend some time learning why the people working on those projects get inspired to come to work in the morning. Develop and present a vision to them of the completed project that hooks into their natural motivations, rather than relying on pure reward/punishment.

Chapter 17
Balancing Management and Leadership
A Growing Business Needs Both Leadership and Management to Thrive

"Management is doing things right; leadership is doing the right things."

— Peter Drucker

The best companies have managers with strong leadership skill and superb management skill. But when chaos strikes, you can't always concentrate on both. (It might even be a luxury to concentrate on *either* for more than an hour at a time!) But what are you losing when you neglect one or the other? Both are essential for keeping a solid foundation during rapid change.

But how?

Use management to adapt processes as the business grows

Management helps the *business* grow. The larger an organization, the more ways things and information flow. As processes become more complex (some would say "sophisticated"), small delays at each step add up to long delays shipping product and serving customers. Well-run projects get neglected, drift off course, and start to drain time and money instead of replenishing them. It's the manager's job to measure, root out the inefficient, prune the irrelevant, and bring errant projects back to the fold.

Managers also guide people by setting up and running the systems that affect people. They set and implement performance evaluations, rewards, and penalties. Managers create rules for employees to live by. Though much of a manager's time is often spent building people systems, the work is about process.

Creating these systems makes growth and change possible. When every business process must be reinvented every time it's needed, forward progress never gets made. The energy that would be moving the business forward is being spent reinventing the present. In the worst case, several people reinvent the same processes in different parts of the business. In one company I worked with, three separate PR agencies managed different product launches, at great expense and great duplication of effort.

Keeping all the systems in place while those very systems will become obsolete in six months is hard. Very hard. Yet it's necessary; work must continue to get done until the company's next growth plateau. But it isn't always clear which tool is best for a given problem. Each tool comes with its own costs and timeframes. Choosing the right tool at a reasonable cost requires careful understanding of the levers that can be used to affect the problem. Fortunately, managers have a huge toolbox to draw from: process mapping, compensation systems, personality assessments for hiring and firing, project management methodologies, finance theory, organization design, etc. Many of those tools can be learned at business schools and taught to help organizations keep their systems running.

Make sure your organization has strong management. Are the big goals clear, measurable, and communicated? Have the systems needed to support those goals been identified and put in place? Do people know how to measure progress to know if they're actually doing anything worthwhile on a day-to-day basis? Make sure your management systems are up to the task every step of the way.

Use Leadership to Bring Out Peoples' Best as the Business Grows

We hate to admit that emotion influences business. In fact, Harvard Business School has only a couple of classes that even acknowledge that emotion exists. Yet most of what happens in business is emotional. Think about the last time you held back giving your "all" on a project. Was it for rational reasons, or because you felt unappreciated/overwhelmed/conflicted? Chances are it was rooted in emotion. The COO of a multi-billion company confided that his biggest agenda items revolved around managing the emotions of his subsidiaries' CEOs. Was he paying attention to their cost controls, or their sourcing strategies, or their IT systems? Of course. But his most important work was on getting them to embrace accountability, an agenda deep in the province of emotion.

If you use management to help business systems grow, you use leadership to help the *people systems grow*. Leadership is not about setting up compensation systems and creating rules. Leading is about touching peoples' identities and emotions: leaders comfort; leaders direct; leaders *inspire*!

In times of change, this is more than just "touchy-feely" and nice-to-have. Change unsettles people. They need a touchstone to stay on track while the world reels around them. That's what a leader provides. When people are looking for guidance, a good leader gives it, confidently. Even if the future is uncertain, the leader offers whatever stability they can to those looking to her for direction.

And they can offer many kinds of stability. They can offer a stable vision of the future that stays constant even when setbacks and surprises sway the course. They can offer *ways of doing business*—values—to anchor people in their process. And when things look hopeless, they can encourage, reassure, and offer hope. These are what bring people to accomplish great things, and this is how a leader becomes the glue that holds a community together during times of threat.

But leadership happens through only a couple of tools. Talking or modeling through their own behavior. That's about it. What not many people realize is that once in a leadership position, they are *always* leading. Every time they talk, and every time they take action, they send signals setting direction and demonstrating what's important—even if that's not what they intend.

Successful leadership is challenging because it is mostly "right brain." It's not so much in *what* you say, but *how you say it*. This kind of subtle communication isn't well-understood. One consulting company hired a Fun Consultant to help revamp the company culture. The kick-off meeting was on an unpaid Saturday, with attendance mandatory for all professional staff. Sound like fun to you? That's what the employees thought, too. Their very culture-building initiative became a symptom of its own failure. Rather than analyzing fun, they could have just gone out and *had* fun. It would have worked a whole lot better.

Adjust your management/leadership balance over time

Companies need management and leadership at different times. When an initiative is just starting out, leadership is paramount. The leader's job, more than anything else, is to inspire other people to believe enough to commit time and resources to an unproven project or company. They are the quintessential team-builder, and typically, with only five or six people working together in a room, management needs are minimal. "Hey, Sam, do we have any prospects we need to call back?" "Yeah. The list is under my bag of M&Ms." Communication is informal, and the shared sense of purpose keeps people on track.

As companies grow, more and more structure begins to creep in. More sales prospects, customers, suppliers, and employees means a lot more organization is needed. Filing cabinets, if nothing else. But especially as the customer base grows beyond the initial friends and early adopters, rapid, repeatable service and quality become important. Management comes to the fore as the organization struggles just to keep doing what it always wanted to do.

Some management systems are needed just to keep things from exploding in chaos. With 200 customers, a good receivables department is needed to keep money flowing in. Other systems are mandated by law. Companies over a certain size must adhere to various human resources policies, worker's compensation requirements, etc.

And there comes a point where the company gets large enough that not everyone is committed anymore. More and more employees consider their job to be "just a job." Branch offices scatter the workforce, and the day-to-day work is routine and procedural. Management has done its work well, but the organization has grown so big that most people's jobs have become small. They see no direct connection between their jobs and the company's health, and certainly no connection between their jobs and the company's direction.

This is when leadership re-enters the picture. While it's nice to think that the right incentive systems, proper rules, and a great Procedures Manual can keep hundreds of people moving in the same direction, it's just not true. It takes a leader to decide where the company is going, and help every member of the company support and feel supported by that vision. The policies manual may say, "Pursue only opportunities with a 15% return on investment," but the leader ties it to emotion: "Pursue opportunities that will make us #1 or #2 in every market we enter." A 15% ROI only inspires an analyst. Being #1 in a market inspires a workforce.

Develop both skill sets... but not necessarily in you

Strong leadership and management will help your organization thrive. But you don't need one person with both skill sets. The skill sets often clash and don't coexist comfortably. Are you good with systems, but not with people? Concentrate on becoming the best manager you can be, and cultivate a partner who is a strong leader. Choose that person for their ability to help you articulate your direction and build a culture that will get you there.

If you're a visionary leader, you already have your vision and your culture. Find a partner who can turn your vision into a rock-solid operation.

Either way, be prepared to manage the balance. A manager's job is to create stability and deal with reality. A leader's job is to stir emotion and set audacious, grandiose goals that shake the status quo. Too much management and you stagnate. Too much leadership and you get nowhere. Embrace the challenge of striking the balance. Do it well, and the results will surpass your wildest dreams.

Chapter 18
Leadership Challenges

"Example is leadership."

— Albert Schweitzer

Challenge #1: Leading a team of older colleagues

Sometimes you don't get the chance to choose your team, and you may end up at a disadvantage when you step up to lead a new team. A common problem is a young leader working with an older team.

Imagine you're Alec, a projects and operations manager at a multinational oil giant in South Africa. You have seven people reporting to you. You're twenty-four years old and the youngest member of the team—the ages range from thirty to forty-three. The team has been working together for the past seven months. You need to gain the genuine trust and respect of your team.

Positional authority is only vaguely useful for getting things done in an organization. The right job title will certainly get people to follow directions, but it won't engage or align them unless they respect and trust you. Respect and trust don't come from an organizational position; they come from building a strong relationship. Trust and respect are intertwined, but distinct; you can give respect without trusting, and you can trust without giving respect.

If you're six years younger than the youngest member of your team, you can't count on gray hair or decades of industry experience to contribute to building respect. You'll have to earn it from scratch.

You can build respect the old-fashioned way: by showing you're really good at what you do. Being the youngest on your team, don't even try to demonstrate the highest technical expertise. Even if you are the best technically, people won't feel great about being out-performed at their own game by someone half their age. They will feel great, however, at having their own strengths magnified by someone who's becoming a really good leader. Build respect by demonstrating excellence at leading.

Ask for help

First things first. Address what no one's talking about: your age. People trust you when they believe you understand them. When you say what everyone is thinking but afraid to say, you'll build trust rapidly. So turn your strength into a weakness. Admit you're in over your head and use it as the foundation for strong relationships. "I'm younger than the rest of the team, yet I'm the manager. We have a job to do as a group. I don't have your industry experience, and I'm counting on you for our success. My job is doing what I can to help *you* create that success. If we all do our part, we'll make a superb team." You're laying the issue on the table and using it to frame a mutual working relationship. Yes, you're young. And that's just a fact. The team can either get over it, pull together, and get the work done, or they can turn it into a problem and stonewall. Either way, once you've had this conversation, you can talk about the choice they've made, rather than silently accepting their implicit reaction.

Now, start helping your team shine. If you make your team members successful as individuals and as a group, you'll earn not only trust and respect, but also that most coveted leadership quality: loyalty.

Set a mission

Teams that shine use each person's strengths to get the greatest results. But before you delve into strengths, you need a team mission to set the direction.

Make sure everyone knows and buys into the mission. The mission is why the group was formed in the first place. If you don't have one, ask the group to help develop the exact wording based on the team's original charter. Have them choose words that are meaningful and emotionally charged to them. What's important is that the mission be more than just nice words. It will be how people know they're doing the right thing. If your team will "develop processes that make existing production more effective" and everyone knows it, they know not to spend time brainstorming new product development. Since a mission is a definition of success, make sure it aligns with your boss's idea of what success means for the team.

Missions and goals may be vague or may become stale over time. That's fine. Notice when they fall short and fix them as needed. Just make sure everyone shares an understanding of the team's current direction. Unless goals are clear, communicated, and agreed upon, you've already lost the battle.

A big part of your job is keeping people aware of the mission. Many new leaders assume that once the team knows what it's supposed to do, all will be well. Nope. Daily work sucks people in and they gradually lose sight of the goal. Remind them often. Use the mission to introduce weekly status meetings, and ask the team to relate their status reports to the team's larger objective.

> **❝** Your job description as a leader is simple: Support your team in whatever they need to meet their goals. **❞**

Figuring out team dynamics

Once you have a common goal, you can start enlisting the team in crafting their working relationship. Age is usually a problem when it comes to job content: when it comes to organizing the process, people care less about age. Take the time to understand each person's unique strengths and blind spots. For each person, challenge the group to ask:

* What are that person's strengths?

* How can that person's strengths contribute to the group?

* What support will that person need from the group to use his strengths most effectively and to compensate for weaker areas?

Include yourself in the discussion. You'll be contributing direction, facilitation, and management. Your strengths don't include decades of industry experience, but that's a good thing; the team can expect you to bring them questions only experience can answer. Likewise, invite them to tell you when their experience contradicts your plans or decisions. With a roadmap of skills and needs, the team provides mutual support toward a common end.

Your job description as a leader is simple: Support your team in whatever they need to meet their goals. Your goal—telling the truth, framing the relationship as mutual support, setting direction, and aligning team members' strengths—builds culture and working relationships. In the day-to-day, your team's need for additional support will change. You'll find yourself acquiring resources, scheduling projects, and shielding people from organizational politics. By occasionally asking, "How can I help you do your job better?" you'll quickly learn how you can help your people succeed.

The more you demonstrate true commitment and honesty, the more people will trust you. The better you do your job, the more the team will respect you. You're doing your job well by honestly addressing the status quo and having the group design working relationships that bring out their best. You may be the only manager in your team members' careers who has taken this approach. They'll respect and trust you for doing what it takes to make *them* successful, and won't care for a moment that you're twenty years their junior.

Challenge #2: Motivating long-term employees who have become apathetic

Another major challenge for leaders is when people get complacent. If you're stepping into a pre-existing company, you may inherit a group of employees who have been there forever and have become apathetic to improving their own lot, space, or environment. But it's possible to help people shift their thinking and practices.

Current wisdom says, "Hire for attitude and train for skills." That's because humans are stubborn, and don't like change. Well, that's not exactly true: We like change when other people are changing to make our lives easier. That's why social change takes a generation—the old mindset has to die off to make room for the new. But all is not hopeless. When attitudes are just a reaction to the work environment, people can change. Fix the situation, show them it's fixed, and let the change begin!

People get cynical and apathetic for good reason. Scandal after scandal reveals golden parachutes, endless perks, and upper managers making millions without linking pay and performance (management by objective seems to stop at the EVP level). Jim Collins says in his book *Good to Great* that there's even evidence that the worse the leader, the more he or she takes home.

But let's assume in your situation that management is prepared to be accountable, will accept a pay level the rank-and-file consider reasonable, and genuinely wants to create a new company culture.

Do as I do

Start with action, not words; people want results, not promises. You'll have to start by delivering change that's in their best interest, and back up your action with words, not the other way around.

A good place to start is by making a visible sacrifice for the company's common good. You might consider cutting your own pay, bonus, and raise—especially if you've had layoffs recently. Give it back to the people who made it: your employees. Increase their benefits, hire back some laid-off workers, or boost salaries. The role model here is Aaron Feuerstein, CEO of Malden Mills, who in 1995 kept 3,000 employees on the payroll after a fire leveled the business. His belief was that his responsibilities extended to employees and the community as well as to shareholders.

Start rewarding those who do a good job now and have done well in the past. Apathy is often rooted in people feeling nothing they do matters. Make it matter! If someone does a good job, do something nice for them! Find out who's done great things in the past but was never recognized. Go thank them for their past contributions. It's probably not appropriate to give them a bonus for what they did before you were on the job, but you can certainly take the team to lunch (your treat) and take a few moments to acknowledge the past oversight.

In addition to rewarding high performers, give *everyone* a sense that showing up for work could make his or her lives better. At first, they won't be able or willing to believe you. You'll have to combat their lack of emotion with added emotion. Find the emotional connection people have with the company.

Some research indicates that people are most motivated when challenged to use their strengths to reach goals they think are do-able.[1] Find emotionally important goals by asking, "What's important about the work you do?" When they answer, ask, "What's important about that? What will that do?" a couple of times. Their answers will reveal values and passions. If they reply, "for the pay," and don't connect with any further goals, they may have no job passion to awaken.

If someone's never had job-related hopes, dreams, or aspirations, he or she probably won't develop them mid-career without some sort of Divine Intervention.

If you have a lot of non-aspirational folks working for you, double-check how you hire. It's easier to change skills than attitudes, so make sure you start hiring people who are more engaged.

But let's assume you have some folks who respond. You see it in their faces; they become animated, or talk with longing in their voices, so you know you've tapped into something real.

Now ask them to stay in that passion, and describe their perfect job. Have 'em go wild. If the past culture has been especially oppressive, you'll probably be amazed at how unwild their dreams actually are. Things like, "having a desk with three drawers" may be a big deal. Ask them, "What one thing can I do to help you move closer to that dream?"

Listen very, very carefully to the answer; you're at a critical moment. They're telling you how you can send an emotional message, not just a verbal one. There may well be no logic to what sends that message. Whatever they say to

---

[1] See *Authentic Happiness* by Marty Seligman, Simon & Schuster 2002.

do, just do it. Say, "I appreciate your sharing that. I'll keep it in mind." Don't promise anything; they've learned that promises get broken. Just quietly get it done. Then check back and ask about next steps. As soon as possible, have them suggest what they can do to drive the change further.

Beware the temptation of self-promotion! Don't crow about how responsive you're being. Make it no big deal. Choose small things and take visible actions that people find meaningful. Actions are what people want, not words. They'll notice, and the word will spread that you're a leader who actually makes life better, rather than issues empty promises.

Once you've taken action and people have evidence that things can be different, it's time to encourage them to step up and do their part. Once they start going, your job is supporting them and helping them align their actions with the direction of the overall company.

This isn't an easy process. If people are truly happy in their work environment, don't expect them to embrace change. But if the apathy comes from bad leadership and unchanging drudgery, you can change that, and they'll get it once you start demonstrating that you're truly different.

Help the change take root

Be vigilant! People will have trouble adapting to you. Even if they're psyched to take the reins, they may need help coping. I worked with a secretary who dreamed of becoming a project manager. When given her first project, she discovered she didn't know how to step up and lead. In meetings, she deferred to senior people out of sheer habit, even when the responsibility was hers as project manager. We worked to help her define her role and to acquire the project management skills to master the position. As a leader, you foster change that may push people into new territory. Be sensitive and be prepared to intervene and help insure their success.

As people take charge, they might charge right in someone else's face. Look out for turf battles, injured egos, feelings of exclusion, and other potential hot spots. When war looks likely, step in and help the participants negotiate a settlement. Get them together, help them find common goals (or remind them of the team's common goals) and then give them the responsibility for working out their differences. Be available as a resource, but get them in the habit of behaving like mature adults. Once you've tapped their motivation, it's up to you to help them grow to work as a strong team that produces solid, substantial results.

Challenge #3: Leadership without authority— Leading a team whose members do not report to you

It's not uncommon for the leader of an organization to depend on people who aren't direct reports. When leading a cross-functional initiative, or co-ordinating across companies with a supplier or client, a good leader needs to motivate people to stay committed to the team and stay focused on the goals established, even though they have other day-to-day work responsibilities.

My first project management job was the Quicken VISA Card. We were creating software to import credit card statements into financial software. The software had to be integrated with five different Intuit products. I had "dotted-line" relationships galore, but no one who actually reported to me. Much of my team had other primary projects, all with separate deadlines. Talk about a disaster waiting to happen.

Leading a team in those circumstances is an ongoing negotiation between you and your team's other priorities. You need to capture your team members' share-of-mind, and keep them wanting to move the project forward. Unlike a direct supervisor, you don't have the tool of authority to help. You'll have to rely on relationships and persuasion.

Easy commitment

Think of your job as helping your team members make your project a priority. You need to know enough about them and their competing commitments so you can work the joint project into their lives. Schedule a one-on-one meeting with each member. Find out what else they're working on, how much time they can commit to the team, and what their big challenges are. Ask about challenges related to their other projects, and spend some time brainstorming ways you can help them on those projects.

> **"** You need to capture your team members' share-of-mind, and keep them wanting to move the project forward. **"**

Don't be afraid to confront the elephant in the room: "Our project isn't your top priority, so how can we insure we make forward progress while helping you complete your other priorities?" Just asking the question shows you care about their priorities. They'll often care about yours in return.

Once you know their other goals, lend them resources. Intervene on their behalf. You heard right: Help them succeed at their competing commitments. The more they fulfill those commitments, the more time they'll have left for you, and the more they'll become committed to your project.

Is one of your team members distracted by a national product launch, for which the logistics are screwed up? Help straighten out the logistics, even though it isn't your job. You would love it if she made you a priority over her other commitments, so demonstrate you're willing to make *her* the priority as well. Do something selfless for her. She'll respond. It just might be the first time someone other than a direct supervisor tried to make her life easier.

Staying in mind

Once you've opened channels of communication, diligently maintain the relationship. As in many relationships, frequency trumps duration: People remember many brief encounters more than a single long one.

Have you ever attended a full-day project kick-off, followed by six months of silence from the project team? That's called "getting off to a resounding thud." When a project starts quietly but comes up daily in conversation, it infiltrates your thinking and becomes part of the culture. That's what you're after. You want your project ever-present in your team members' minds.

But you want it to be present in a good way. Make sure each project-related contact leaves people feeling like it was a good use of time. That means finding excuses to interact that aren't "status meetings." Most people dislike status meetings. Personally, I despise them. For frequent-but-brief contacts, connect to provide value to your team members and use as little of their time as possible. Contact them with help, with direction they need, with resources, or with one-on-one requests for status. Remember: Your goal with these contacts is simple awareness.

In addition to awareness, a team for a large project may need to feel a team identity. Do that separately. I believe teamwork should happen naturally, not through off-sites and ropes courses. From your early meetings and ongoing relationship-building, you'll understand what your team members need and what they contribute. Facilitate their working together, so they build respect for each other as part of getting the work done. Find opportunities for them to help each other and match them up at those times. "Hmm, Sandy, you need help with the bar graph tool? Did you know that Aaron was working on it just last week?" If team cohesion is a real issue, ask them if they would like formal team-building meetings. At all times, let them drive the process in a way that works given their other commitments.

Put your project in context

If people in your organization are generally committed to the goals of the overall organization, you can strengthen commitment to your project by helping them understand how the project fits into the company's larger goals. For instance, if the company is branching out into new markets with your project, you can help the team understand that the project is strategically important, and not just busy work.

When you're meeting with team members to understand their concerns, ask questions to uncover anything that would hinder their ability to work on your project:

- What other projects are you working on?

- How much time will you have to devote to this project?

- What opportunities does this project provide to help you advance in the company?

- What resources can I help you obtain that will free up time for you to work on the joint project?

- What suggestions do you have for making our project successful?

Similarly, if there is an executive whose organization spans both your project and your teams' areas, you might want to ask the executive to talk at a team meeting, to reinforce how much the project matters to the organization.

Appealing to company goals is powerful in a healthy environment, but should be done with caution if morale is low. In some companies (often those with histories of layoffs or unfair treatment), people view the company and its success very cynically. Appealing to company goals won't be motivating. In many companies, however, people feel loyalty to and care about the company. They'll be motivated to help the business reach its goals.

There's no perfect answer to managing a team with other commitments. But if you take the time to make it easy for your team members to contribute, keep your project top-of-mind, and help them understand how important it is, you'll have the best chance of pulling together a team that can get the job done even amidst challenges and distractions.

Chapter 19
Taking Responsibility as a Leader

"The price of greatness is responsibility."

— Sir Winston Churchill

We all love to take credit when things go right and shift the blame when things go wrong. It's especially tempting as a leader. The leader is perfectly positioned to blame just about anyone and anything when things go wrong. "The market is down." "That clerk in accounting is incompetent." "We didn't count on competition." "Regulation is unfair." "The legal department reviewed it before I said it." Such quotes avoid responsibility, and whether from fear or insecurity, they herald the beginning of the fall from leader to pretender.

Recently, a top executive at a Fortune 500 firm announced to his general managers that a major initiative had been a mistake. He thanked everyone for their hard work, and then laid it on the line. He said, "This decision was mine." He outlined the thinking that led to the decision. He highlighted assumptions he had made and bets he had taken. "I was simply wrong. You have done an excellent job supporting this decision, and nothing you could have done would have helped. My job is to give you quality process and make the right decision. In this case, the decision was wrong. We're canceling the initiative and starting over." He received a standing ovation. Even multi-decade veterans of the company had never before heard a senior manager openly take responsibility for failure.

Responsibility is an action verb

As a leader, you must take responsibility. "Take" is the operative word; embrace responsibility. When things go wrong, if your first instinct is to look for someone to blame, stop. Ask instead, "What can I do to help fix this?" Then do it. That's taking responsibility. Only when you've gotten things back on the right track should you consider blame.

But blame's a funny thing. Who is to blame for layoffs? "The competitive situation?" I think not. The largest line item in most income statements is salary. It's the job of senior management to manage their income statement over the long term. The unwritten contract when hiring someone to work on an initiative is that the company will preserve any jobs created, unless it's explicitly agreed otherwise. Poor account planning could be blamed on external forces, sure. But you know what? It could also be blamed on bad long-term planning. The blame may somehow belong externally, but placing it there doesn't help the organization get better. So pretend the blame is yours and explore what you could do to make it right.

Do what's under your control

You can only get better at what's under your control. One great thing about leadership in our economy is that we get bonuses, salary, and tons of money when things go right, even if they are outside our control. A CEO friend of mine worth $60 million confided that she has absolutely no idea what she's doing. She thinks she was simply in the right place at the right time. Lucky for her! But with riches-for-results comes the flip side: when things go wrong—for whatever reason—taking responsibility is just as important.

Responsibility means, literally, "the ability to respond." If you're a leader in your organization, you have the ability to respond before, during, and after a crisis. So start by placing the blame on yourself. Spend five minutes feeling awful. Pull your hair out. Feel like a failure. Seriously contemplate suicide. Fantasize that your spouse will divorce you and you'll die in a gutter befriended only by rats (it could happen). Then get over yourself and ask questions that will lead you to become better and better at what you do.

What could you have done that you didn't do? Think about the crisis. What could you have done beforehand to avert it? What event would have tipped you off that you needed to take that action? Can you apply that lesson in the future? You may find that spending more time doing quality assurance on your product was called for. Or perhaps you should have spent more time building that critical customer relationship.

What could you not have done that you did do? Review your actions before and during the crisis. Which of your actions reinforced the crisis, prevented it from being averted, or directly caused it? Perhaps it wasn't the wisest course of action to announce to your shareholders at your annual meeting, "We don't believe a company should be managed for the shareholders." (True story... I was there.) Or maybe you should have taken your right-hand-person's advice when they suggested changing course.

What interpretations did you make that you could have made differently? It isn't just action that gets in the way. Your interpretation of events, of people's communication, of market forces, or of competitive moves may have led to the problem. Review your interpretations and decide whether you need to do some updating. That dip in sales may have been because people really don't want to buy your new chocolate covered machine parts. It may have nothing to do with the decision to use milk chocolate instead of dark.

These questions make great debriefing questions for you. And they also make great debriefing questions for your teams. Using this framework to begin a crisis post-mortem will help build an organization that learns, rather than blames. It may not be as comfy as denial, but it's better for survival.

This is hard stuff, but people's lives depend on your decisions. That's serious! So when things go wrong, own them. Learn from them. Step up and respond as best as you're able. Sometimes you'll fall short, or won't know what to do. Welcome to the human race. It's not about being perfect: it's about being responsible when you aren't perfect. Set a standard of responsibility for everyone around you, and at the end of the day, you'll not only have built a business, you'll have built a rewarding life. It's your choice, and your responsibility.

Chapter 20
Balance Rights with Responsibilities
Creating Your Bill of Responsibility

"Rights that do not flow from duty well performed are not worth having."

— Mahatma Gandhi

Do you have a personal Bill of Responsibility as a business leader? It's an intriguing concept. Allow me to explain...

In America, we businesspeople happily ask a lot from our employees. We all accept the need for unpaid "crunch time" before a deadline, even though "crunch time" means we failed as project managers. And does "crunch time" become less common over time? Rarely. That's also on our shoulders; we business leaders are responsible for the failure to learn. But we expect employees to give from their personal lives to compensate for a company's poor management.

But we rarely hold ourselves to as high a standard. We shake our heads mournfully and say, "Sorry you aren't getting that raise I promised... sales were off, and budgets are tight." Most employees accept that "business realities" come first. We are accountable to shareholders for earnings, but when was the last time an executive was fired for breaking promises to employees? If an employee spent too much on their new entertainment center and they ask for more money, would we give it? Of course not! At best, we'd offer a session with a financial manager and tell them to manage their cash better in the future. Yeah, right. Just as we so deftly managed our resources to avoid "crunch time."

Our country is founded on the notion of personal rights. We even have a Bill of Rights in our Constitution. Businesses take for granted a far wider set of rights than people. What's missing is the other half of that equation: the Bill of Responsibilities. Leadership doesn't come from exercising your rights; it comes from fulfilling your responsibilities, and doing it with honor. And it comes from having a set of responsibilities that the people around you respect—the kind that make you an example worth following.

Put it into action:

- Write down your Bill of Responsibilities. Not the things you're legally obligated to do, but the things that you feel a Good Leader should do for the people in their organization.

- How are you doing? On a scale from 1 to 10, are you fulfilling your responsibilities?

- How are you *really* doing? On a scale from 1 to 10, how would your employees and group members say you're doing?

- If you're below a 10 on some of your responsibilities, commit to an action or two a week you can take to fulfill that responsibility. Track it in your daily planner, and really make it happen.

- If you're a 10 on all scales, your challenge for the week is to raise your standards. You've shown you can do it; now do it better.

Chapter 21
Motivating through Expectation
Bring Out Your Team's Best by Setting Expectations—Yours!

"Outstanding leaders go out of the way to boost the self-esteem of their personnel. If people believe in themselves, it's amazing what they can accomplish."

— *Sam Walton*

Who have been the leaders in your life? The people who expected you to give your best, and usually knew you could do far more than you imagined. They didn't do it by demeaning you and putting you down, either. They did it by expecting your best in ways that transcend their demands: they asked you to surpass your limits, and somehow in their presence, you did. It's no coincidence. Positive expectations are powerful, and you can use them to help those around you break through their own barriers.

When you stay in a Ritz-Carlton, you expect the best in service. But it's more than an expectation—you're demanding great performance. If that rose isn't right on your pillow, you'll give 'em heck! Demands rarely bring out someone's best. Demands are about you and your wishes, not about *them*. But underlying your Ritz expectations is faith that the Ritz can deliver superb service. The faith is so deep you don't even question it. And it's that faith that produces the magic.

Do you have the same faith about everyone who works for you? And I do mean *everyone*.

You see, the "Pygmalion Effect" is very real and very potent. When told their students are gifted, teachers find their classes perform exceptionally, even when the students actually tested normal before entering the class. Expectations affect teachers' eye contact, patience with student difficulties, time spent with students, facial expressions, etc. Those all conspire to fulfill the expectation of gifted performance.

Whatever expectations do, they go deeper than conversation. Expectations don't even require human subjects—the original Pygmalion study was done on rats. In 1968, Harvard Professor Robert Rosenthal gave super-intelligent rats to researchers and watched the rats behave at those levels. The rats, however, were actually "normal" rats. Somehow, researchers were coaxing amazing performance from the rats—based on the researchers' expectations, not the rats' histories.

Now research shows most first impressions are formed in 5-30 seconds. That's scary! Two minutes into a conversation, we've already made an evaluation, which, by virtue of the Pygmalion effect, easily becomes a self-fulfilling prophecy.

Face it: you're going to form self-fulfilling prophecies based on a near-total lack of data. So why not do it in ways that bring out the best in everyone around you? Start using Pygmalion deliberately. In Rosenthal's lab, it was rats. In our business and lives, it can be employees, team members, and bosses. Consider where you've had trouble with employees. Do you have a team member you expect to be troublesome? Incompetent? Unruly? Notice how you behave next time you're together. Notice how you interpret their actions. Notice your thoughts. Are you saying to yourself, "Jeez, there goes Arnash again, always bragging"? You'll notice that your response is based on your interpretation, not their actions.

Once you're safely away, replay the scene in your mind. But first, imagine that the person is someone you deeply respect and admire. Play the scene with them engaging in the same behavior, and notice what you think this time. Are you interpreting differently, "Hmm... Arnash seems insecure today. Maybe I should say something positive." You'll be surprised how different expectations really produce different results.

Expectations play a role in how we deal with bosses, Boards of Directors, investors, customers, etc. A small software startup viewed their investors as basically critics, and kept communication to a minimum. Largely in the dark, investors couldn't lend support or advice when disasters struck. Ultimately, investors became quite critical of management, and the initial expectation was fulfilled.

Other startups treat investors as a part of their resource team. They keep investors in the loop, turn to them for aid, and find that most investors are happy to contribute to make a venture succeed. While relationships rise or fall for many reasons, expectations can go a long way in helping or hurting.

Expecting the best doesn't mean you blindly trust or overlook incompetence. What you're after is a mindset that truly brings out the other person's best. Sometimes, you'll find their best just doesn't cut it. In those cases, do what you must. But holding good intentions throughout will give them and you the best chance of success.

Start shaping your expectations to bring out the best in everyone around you. Your life will change totally. Expect it.

Putting it into action:

- Who do you have faith in, enough so you consistently expect the best?

- Who is so mediocre you just tolerate, but would like to inspire instead?

- Spend 30 seconds imagining, in as much detail as possible, how you would treat your Tolerate person if you truly believed they wanted to perform at their best and were able to follow through.

- Consider one, then the other, noticing the differences in how you think about each one.

- Start thinking of the first person. Slowly superimpose the second person's image over the first, having it get clearer and clearer until you're looking at the second person's image. Do it only as quickly as you hold on to the feelings of faith. Then clear your mind and do it a couple more times until you think of the second person with the same high expectations backed by faith in their abilities.

- Check in a week from now. How did your expectations change your relationship?

Extra challenge

Find places in your personal life where you could bring out the best in those around you, simply by having faith in them and their abilities. (Hint: If you can't think of anyone, what about friends? children? in-laws?)

Chapter 22

Make Lots of Mistakes; Just Make Sure They're New Ones

Failure Doesn't Guarantee Learning, Just the Chance to Learn!

"Leadership and learning are indispensable to each other."

— John F. Kennedy

A friend of mine was a dot-com CEO during the painful death spiral of the early 2000s. He shared the story: "It was painful, but I learned a lot." Eager to learn without suffering the pain myself, I asked, "What did you learn?" He rattled off five superficial lessons that most college freshman could guess with a moment's thought. Only in my friend's case, it cost $100 million of investor's money and four years for him to learn those lessens. There's gotta be a cheaper way. We say we learn from our mistakes, but few of us really extract quality learning from our experience. If you're going to make mistakes, make them thoroughly, and learn well from them.

Schedule time for learning. Don't assume learning happens automatically; it usually doesn't. We learn to recognize familiar patterns without giving it much attention, but deeper learning requires reflection and thought. People often skip learning, saying, "We have urgent things to do. There's no time to do a project review." What silliness! You can do a good review in a single day. If you learn one lesson that can save you two days during the next project, then the review pays for itself in spades!

Schedule time for yourself (and/or your team) to reflect on your experience. Take steps to insure you get the most from your learning.

Pretend bad news was all your fault. You can always blame customers, employees, or the market. "We're doing poorly because times are tough." Don't fall for this cop out! It may be true, but it doesn't help you succeed—it just cultivates a victim mentality. Ask, "What decisions could we have made to succeed, even given the tough times?" If $100 million can't get my friend's company to profitability in four years, it's a statement about management, not "the market."

The world is mostly outside your control, but you always contribute to the situation. Start asking what *you* could have done differently. What did you do that you shouldn't have? What did you not do that you should have? And how did your interpretation of events, actions, and motivations contribute to the outcome? Success lies in ruthless examination of your part in your business's unfolding drama.

Learn from specific experience, not ad hoc memory. If you try to list lessons off the top of your head, you'll overemphasize recent experience and emotional events. Instead, map out significant events and decision points on a timeline. List the assumptions you made. Then start noticing how events led to the end result. From there, you can extract high quality learning.

For instance, if your timeline shows:

Jan 1   Hired new VP of Sales. Assumption: she will be able to generate $5 mm in sales this year

Feb 15   Management offsite to finalize company positioning statement

May 22   Fortune 100 prospect fell through. Assumption: we assumed that the customer simply changed their mind. (Found out in September that they bought from someone else!)

Jun 10   Three-day offsite to discuss below-expected sales

Jun 30   No Q2 bonuses, due to low sales

Aug 5   Bank balance hit zero

You may be tempted to conclude your VP of Sales was a bozo. Maybe she was. But examining the timeline may uncover a richer set of learning questions:

- Which sales strategies worked? which didn't?
- Which product positioning didn't work?
- Should your hiring criteria for Sales VP be changed?
- Was executive compensation linked to performance?
- Did you oversee and manage your executive properly?

Decisions are a rich source of learning. Examine how you made decisions. Were they framed as "either-or" when, in retrospect, there were many more alternatives? Did you use good criteria, or did you use gut feel combined with the need to take some action, because things were in a panic? If you can mine your decisions for good lessons, you can improve your future effectiveness dramatically.

Turn Learning into Action

While a sheet of paper titled "Lessons Learned" looks really nice and sexy, it won't change your actions unless you put the lessons into practice. For each major learning, identify something you can do differently from what you've done in the past. Then do it! And then take the next step. And so on.

Change is hard because we're built to feel comfortable when things are familiar. "Familiar" is the key. We feel better failing in a familiar way than succeeding in an unfamiliar way. A client of mine realized that successfully leading a company meant letting go of details he'd previously mastered and spending more time on strategy. His brain knew he should make the shift, but the strategy work felt weird and unfamiliar to him. He kept lapsing back into the details, alienating his employees and, frankly, wasting his time in one fell swoop.

But never fear: practice breeds familiarity. Once you know how you need to act differently, start doing it at every opportunity. If you're as big a measurement junkie as I am, make a tracking sheet so each day you can map your progress over time.

Putting it into action: go do some high-quality learning!

- Schedule a half-day, right now, to review a past project or decision. Good or bad, choose something you haven't yet taken the time to consider in detail. This works best if you involve the whole team that had a stake in the outcome. For extra credit, choose a situation where you were the victim of the market, the dot-com crash, etc., etc., etc. For extra-extra credit, choose a situation where you lost more than $10,000,000 of other people's money.

- On a huge whiteboard, map out the timeline of events leading to the outcome. Err on the side of including anything that might be vaguely relevant.

- Scan the events and develop a large set of learning questions in which you challenge the assumptions you held, the actions you took, the actions you didn't take, and the interpretations you put on events. Assume you could affect everything, even if you chose not to exercise your input.

- Explore the learning questions with your team. Draw out guidelines for acting differently in the future.

- If any of those guidelines will come into play in the near future, identify the specific triggers that will signal you it's time to use the new learnings. Agree amongst the group to help each other implement the new learning.

- Repeat until learning reviews become familiar.

Chapter 23
Propagating Learning through Organizational Change

"Those who do not learn from history are doomed to repeat it."

— American Proverb

With so much riding on success, you would think that companies would embrace learning when you lay out the need for it. People should jump to participate. Right? We wish! Amazingly, it seems as if people fight tooth and nail against learning, often with disastrous results. The reasons, however, make a lot of sense. And once you understand the reasons, you just might be able to make a difference. If not, at least you can feel self-righteous when the insanity starts.

First of all, we know learning takes time, but it's hard to persuade people to put it on the schedule. They didn't used to need to, you know. Once upon a time, reflection time was built into the world. It took three weeks for a head-office communication to arrive via Pony Express, allowing ample time to ponder and rethink decisions. Now we have overnight letters, junk mail, e-mail, voice mail, faxes, cell phones, 30-second-delayed stock quotes, and the expectation that responding *immediately* is far more important than responding thoughtfully.

In an organization that doesn't build in time for thoughtful learning, reflection is the first victim when emergencies beckon. When we built the original Quicken VISA card, we scheduled a learning debrief and documentation time. But long before the project's end, other demands squeezed all the slack out of the schedule. The learning review was the first to go. If you don't do it deliberately, learning won't happen.

Your first challenge is getting people to carve out time for learning. If they won't do it on a per-project basis, be sneaky. Schedule a quarterly off-site, or piggy back on an existing group meeting that's usually a waste of time. (If all your meetings are 100% effective, then by all means, lay the ground work by having two or three off-sites that are a waste of time. Then choose those.) Just find a time people are willing to block out. Then surprise them—instead of the usual agenda, spring learning on them. Review the previous quarter, rather than a specific project, but get them used to doing some learning. Take special care to involve people from around the company, so everyone has something to contribute and everyone can walk away with quality learning. Facilitate carefully, keeping in mind the goal is to give them the experience that a day spent learning can save even more time later.

Implementing insights from a learning summit can be tough if it involves organizational behavior change. Even though it's a much-discussed topic, organizational change is rightly daunting.

Think about what organizational change is: It's changing structure and processes. At the very least, a lot of people must change how they work. Responsibilities, roles, and reporting relationships change. And that's just in the easy case; learning that your phone system is the bottleneck in your customer service department may demand reworking physical plant and equipment in several locations. Getting the affected people together to coordinate can take weeks. Then new systems must be designed, built, and documented, and everyone must be taught how their jobs have changed. Then there's still a learning curve for the new procedures. People get up to speed at the new ways of doing things, and only then has the business "learned." And, oh yes, this all happens in spare time, because the normal workload is still present and has to be carried for the business to survive.

" Organizations rarely build in time to do thoughtful learning. "

Part of changing the systems and structure is changing the people. A reorg can be done on paper in an afternoon. But changing just one person is hard, even when he or she understands the need for change (Yes, my doctor said to lower my intake of saturated fats, but those cookies at lunch yesterday were so good I just had to eat … six … of them). Ultimately, organizational learning is doomed to failure unless people can learn.

For starters, a lot of learning breaks down because it's never communicated. Telling someone "Now you report to Sally and your department is no longer sales, it's account relationships" still leaves them to figure out how their day-to-day job has changed. They weren't necessarily privy to the learning discussions, and can't do anything meaningful without more information about the changes and the context.

Context answers the question "Why is this happening?" It's especially important when motivating people. People like things to stay the same. But when we find out *why* the request was made, it suddenly makes sense. Without knowing the "Why?" most change just makes life difficult with no obvious payoff… thus, resistance.

Even if people understand the changes, they may not have the skills for the new job. When Microsoft learned that security matters to customers, Bill Gates proclaimed that all programmers would spend two months just fixing security problems. A great goal, to be sure, but the programmers had spent their careers building systems without regard to security. How can we expect them to suddenly develop the expertise to find—much less fix—any but the simplest security flaws?

> **" One recalcitrant manager with the right budget authority can halt a learning effort in its tracks. "**

And as with any change effort, Microsoft is starting with workers who uniformly lack the skills being developed. Over time, organizational priorities shape the work force. Security-conscious engineers never had a chance to develop their skills at Microsoft, so if they really cared they left years ago for companies more aligned with their style. Those who stayed are the ones who thrive in the "get it out the door and capture the market" mentality. So the change is starting with the employees least likely to intuit how the changes should happen.

Money can come to the rescue by training people. For a simple skill, it can be quick and easy. But training for large skills must be developed, delivered, and practiced. No matter how much we "thrive on chaos" and "jump into the vortex," new habits take time to develop. A long time. Humans only change at a certain rate and we've never figured out how to speed that up. The world may change faster than ever, but people just don't.

The ones who most need to change, however, are the managers. As the organization reshapes itself, resources will shift. That means money and people. Budgets will get slashed. Empires will topple. Even if everyone else is willing, one recalcitrant manager with the right budget authority can halt a learning effort in its tracks. Managers must let go and support the learning for it to happen. Being human, they can have as much difficulty changing their behavior as everyone else.

By now, I've probably convinced you that organizational learning is hopeless. But take heart: now that you know why learning is hard, you can deliberately make it easier.

Steps to Make Learning Easier	Example
1. Schedule time for learning. Make learning an explicit part of your job, rather than something you hope happens. Choose an issue to address.	Our vendors are refusing to take new orders. When we asked why, they said, "chronically late payment."
2. Here's the big secret: decisions are at the heart of organizational behavior. Even if you only have time for one thing, learn by asking your group, "What decisions must be made differently as a result of our experience, and how will those decisions need to change?"	We must decide that vendor payment is a priority. When setting out the week's tasks, vendor payment must be scheduled first.
3. Express the learning as how you want the organization to behave differently. Be specific.	From now on, Accounts Payable will cut a check three days before the due date on a bill.
4. Understand the organizational implications of the new learning. What systems and structures must change for the learning to manifest?	The AP files must be updated and reviewed daily. "Due upon receipt" bills must be entered immediately instead of weekly.
5. Move from organizational implication to personal implications. Whose behavior will change? How will it change? What requests will be made of them that aren't being made now?	Pat must read and process incoming mail daily. Chris must process checks daily instead of weekly.
6. Even if it isn't your job, take responsibility for helping people understand why the change is necessary. Help them identify the skills they will need to deal with the job changes. Encourage them to find ways to develop those skills, even if training isn't available.	Chris may need new time-management skills.
7. Work with the managers whose employees are affected to direct money, people, and time in support of the learning.	Chris's manager and Chris must make sure that his new mix of responsibilities still makes sense.

Organizational learning isn't easy. There's no perfect solution. Despite the many reasons why learning is hard for individuals and even harder for organizations, it's just a behavior that can become a habit. Develop the learning habit. Practice moving learning into individual action. Help people change and grow. Over time, the very forces that make change hard will come to your aid: those who don't like learning will gradually leave, and you'll attract a culture of people committed to learning. Even when an organization fights it, strong, dedicated action can at least produce pockets of smart business savvy.

Chapter 24

"Losses" and Responsibility

How Everyday Business Language Lets Us Engage In Deception

"Nothing is more common on earth than to deceive and be deceived."

— Johann G. Seume

When you're changing your organization, pay close attention to your words. We seem to be living in the century of spin. We don't fire people, we don't even lay them off, and we often don't even downsize. We "right-size." There's a verbal cop-out if I've ever heard one. But if you watch your language even more closely, you'll find normal business-speak misdirects responsibility.

Worldcom announced $4 billion in losses that had been buried as, um, capital expenditures. (Oops. Don't you just hate it when that happens?) Enron collapses from horrendous mismanagement, taking Arthur Anderson down for obstruction of justice. Tyco apparently funneled billions of company dollars straight to the founder's family. Global Crossing... Xerox... Merck... . Everyone is so upset about the losses. We're losing so much money. Losses, losses everywhere. But wait!

What does that mean? When I "lose" my wallet, it's because it got accidentally (and thoughtlessly) misplaced. Getting into the cab, it was there. Six tequila shots later, when it was time to pay, the wallet was gone. Whoops. I must have lost it. Fortunately, the realization comes after the six shots, so the consequences (while probably severe) seem like little more than a hazy dream.

Newspapers report that in the mid-90s, Worldcom's management "built" a telecommunications giant. When Worldcom acquired MCI, MCI was a company with a multi-decade track record, three times the size of Worldcom. As Worldcom collapses, it will take MCI with it. That's not building a giant. That's playing funky accounting tricks and destroying tens of billions of dollars worth of viable companies. Worldcom management didn't build anything at all.

But hey, they cry, "Telecomm competition heated up and we lost money." No, they didn't. They didn't "lose" money at all.

It's one thing to say I lost my wallet. It's another thing entirely to say a company loses money. Companies know exactly where their money goes. They spend billions tracking it. Does a CEO stand up before the board and proclaim with a goofy grin, "Gee, I had $142 million when getting into the cab, but it was gone when we got to dinner"? Nope. Every cent that left that company did so with the approval and signature of a company employee. **The money wasn't lost, it was wasted**. Or stolen. Or given to executives, or simply mismanaged.

We understand that a late-90s Internet CEO might truly have misplaced $142 million dollars on the way back from a Really Cool Nightclub. After all, wearing dark sunglasses at night *does* make it hard to keep track of a checkbook.

But when discussing Fortune 500 companies like Merck, Worldcom, or Enron, we start by assuming competence. Bad idea. Perhaps it would help us keep in mind our fiduciary responsibilities if companies stopped reporting "losses" and started reporting "wastages" or "bad money managementages."

So:

> "GenericCo today reported losses of $3 million. Company executives blame the loss on market forces."

becomes:

> "GenericCo today reported bad money management of $3 million dollars. Company officials blame the loss on market forces."

Kind of makes doublespeak a bit harder, doesn't it? But it still puts all the attention on the blame, rather than the learning. And though that is certainly the most common emphasis, it doesn't help us grow or get better. How about this kinder, gentler version:

> "GenericCo today reported management learning opportunities of $3 million. Company officials blame the loss on the market forces."

I like it. It makes it clear who should be making sure such things don't happen, and as long as they aren't actually foolish enough to add the sound bite about "market forces," it leaves the reader realizing that having more expenses than income is, in fact, a learning opportunity.

Another fun trick is to speak as if we had nothing to do with an outcome. "The project is late." Uh-huh. The project and Mr. Invisible got together to sabotage the project. Try, "We missed four milestones and weren't willing to recognize the danger until two days before our scheduled ship date." It doesn't sound as sexy, but maybe if you phrase things that way, you'll do something about them next time.

Yes, our language lets us avoid responsibility. And it makes us much more comfy; we needn't face up to our own imperfections. But powerful leaders embody integrity. Integrity and learning both require taking a hard, objective look at facts. If they're embarrassing, you can keep the observations to yourself, but if you use doublespeak to fool yourself, you won't fool anyone else. You'll also stunt your learning, making it harder to reach true excellence.

Putting it into action:

* Substitute "management learning opportunity" for "losses" in your language across the board. If you hear yourself saying, "We had quarterly management learning opportunities of $3 million. We blame the market," give a chuckle and find a way to rephrase that. For learning to happen, it's gotta come first from you.

* When you hear someone (even yourself) talking about inanimate objects as if they're responsible for business results, rephrase to put the action where it belongs. Find out how that changes what you'll do next.

* Find other places you use doublespeak to make uncomfortable accountability easier to handle. Substitute "learning doublespeak" that orients you toward the learning, rather than emotional evasion.

* Celebrate. You're on your way to higher integrity, higher learning, and becoming a more powerful inspiration to those around you.

Chapter 25
Conquering the Stress
of Uncertainty
Keeping Yourself Sane in Times of Uncertainty

"The only certainty is that nothing is certain."

— Pliny the Elder

The reason leaders have integrity, an unwavering vision, and solid, motivating values is to be the anchor when everyone feels tossed by circumstance. But who is the rock for the leader? Economic slowdowns, changes in technology, and a dozen other factors have changed our world making the future less secure and less predictable than it once was. We can no longer count on steady growth and reliable money. It's easy to become stressed when we aren't seeing the results we expect.

In Western culture, we're not taught coping skills for uncertainty. It can be especially hard having patience and a clear mind when things aren't going the way we want them to (witness our country's difficulty with two weeks of uncertainty around our Y2K Presidential election!).

If you haven't been seeing success right away, start by asking yourself "what constitutes success?" If you're attached to an outcome—say, doing $10 million of sales in your first year—you'll find that success is all-or-nothing; you've either reached the outcome or you haven't. It may help you feel progress to subdivide your goal into smaller pieces. Shoot for at least one milestone a week, so your progress is continuous. Your first week's goal could be to get a face-to-face appointment with three prospects and land one sale. Each goal you meet will help you feel progress.

The key is that you're not choosing your milestones just to manage the projects. This is about managing your emotions. Choose milestones that will cause you to feel progress in your gut, even if the outside results aren't there yet.

You can also succeed with process goals. Process goals measure what you're doing, not where you are. You're shooting for three prospect appointments? You might set a process goal of calling 10 Widget Retailers from the phonebook daily. That's a process goal. If you find you're missing your process goals, asking yourself why can lead to you choosing a better way to reach your outcome. For example, if you miss your 10 daily calls because there are only three Widget Retailers in the phone book, it's a signal that you'll need another way to find prospects. Process goals give you the chance for daily "wins" on your way to your bigger goals.

If you find yourself stressed even when you reach smaller progress goals, you might want to tackle the stress directly. Meditate for a half hour a day, get some exercise, and set aside time for yourself to relax and unwind. Choose a time for the day to be over and when it is, go home and do something completely unrelated to work. It can be a challenge, but separating work and home life can save your sanity. At least three times a week, leave your office by 6 p.m. and go play. Clear your mind. Get a massage. Indulge yourself in a bubble bath. Treat yourself well! (My personal touchstone is yoga.)

Of course, it's possible your business might not be truly sustainable. The market may not be there, the distribution can't be worked out, or competition makes it impossible to build a business that makes money. Set boundaries for yourself to keep yourself healthy. Decide now how much time/money/effort you are willing to put into the business, so you don't someday wake up having overspent yourself. Also, think hard on how you'll know if the business really won't work. Just setting those limits can help. If you decide three months of consecutive losses is the signal that your specialty Pokeman Roller Skate Shop has outlived its usefulness, then you'll know when it's time to quit. And knowing there's a defined exit point can really be calming.

But meanwhile, give it your all! With well-thought-out process and outcome goals, you may never have to worry about your exit conditions. You'll know early on if what you're doing isn't working, and you can take action to insure your success. With hard work, skill, and a little luck, your main worries will be plotting your multibillion-dollar expansion... as you relax in your mansion's new whirlpool bubble bath.

Part 3

Staying Organized, Focused, and Sane

"A time management seminar? I don't have time to go to that thing!"

Chapter 26
The Power of Focus Time
A Terrifying Way to Make Sure You'll Actually Get Stuff Done This Week

"The ability to concentrate and to use time well is everything."

— *Lee Iacocca*

So you've built your organization. You have vision. You're doin' the leadership thing. You stride happily into your office, move to sit down, and your phone rings. You answer, and a call wait comes in. You put your first call on hold, greet your second caller, as your eye catches the instant message that pops up saying, "We're about to lose the Henderson contract." You groan inwardly, and your assistant pokes a head in the door and mimes "There's an emergency. Come NOW!" It's fun to be boss.

At the end of the day, all the great strategy and leadership comes down to getting stuff done. And in a world of hyper-overload, that's a tall order. Fortunately, there's a simple, extremely effective technique for making mega-progress on a project. Be warned: it's simple, and to most of us, it's terrifying.

Expect to scream in horror. You'll laugh in denial. In your shock, you will retreat into rationalization: "That's impossible. I just couldn't do that. Stever just doesn't understand... ." But if you follow today's advice, you will be in for a major transformation.

Let's ease into it. The 50,000-foot strategy is simple: create focus time. We often get bogged down because we just don't spend enough time in "flow" on a project. Interruptions happen. We have too many other projects demanding our time. E-mail, phone calls, pagers, office workers, idle thoughts, overheard conversations all distract us. Just a little bit, but the little bits add up and at the end of the day, it's common to find out that we've done less of the Big Important stuff than we wanted. But focusing on the important is much easier said than done.

The first step in focus is to decide you'll do it. That's the hardest part. If you're ready to make the commitment to yourself, read on. Otherwise, consider trying it for a week. If you have trouble with that level of commitment, stop reading and spend some time really exploring why you're so sure you can't do it. Then try again.

Once you've decided to focus, decide how long you need in each sitting. For example, four hours, which is how long it takes me to build real momentum on a project. Then block out that much time on your schedule. Daily. Starting the week after next.

"What??? That's absurd! I can't block out *four hours* a day on my schedule!" I hear you cry.

Bull-pucky.

If you're so gosh-darned important that you're in such demand, then you're important enough to create the space to perform up to your Excellence. Block out four hours a day as an "interruption-free zone." Your sudden scarcity will make you that much more desirable in the minds of your co-workers. Besides, we both know you'll cheat and schedule last-minute important things in the middle of one or two of those four-hour blocks. So by reserving five 4-hour blocks, you stand a good chance of honoring two or three in any given week.

Then assign a project to each time block. Make sure to rotate projects enough that over a week or two, you make progress on all your projects. Here are some guidelines for your interruption-free zone:

- If you have a gatekeeper (admin assistant), make sure they know you're not to be disturbed for anything except an emergency.

- Close your office door. If you live in a cubicle, put up a sign saying, "Do not disturb. Excellence in progress." If you don't even have a cubicle, tape a sign to your back.

- Isolate yourself from noise. Put on headphones if necessary, with a CD that will promote your ability to concentrate. Turn off your phone.

- Isolate yourself from electronic distractions. If your email is set to automatically notify you of new email, turn off the notification or shut down the email program entirely. Close chat windows and instant messenger. Turn off your cell phone, pager, desk phone, and Blackberry™.

- Get into the flow, roll up your sleeves, and jump on in!

Keeping Your Boundaries During Focus Time

Two powerful forces will be fighting against your focus time: you and everyone else. Set firm boundaries, and don't let them break your stride.

You'll most likely disturb yourself by remembering "important" things you just can't live without handling right now. Keep a pad near you to record "stuff to do when done focusing." When you are tempted to switch attention, write down the distraction on that pad and then deal once your focus time is over.

If others disturb you, explain that you're in the middle of your focus time, which is necessary for you to make progress on large projects. Ask them to send you email, or tell them you will call them back after your focus time is over (or when you reach a breaking point). People will grumble, but then they'll do as you ask, secretly envying your ability to create the space you need for achievement.

Is this really possible?

Yes. It's hard. I know the principle and only do it around 30% as much as I'd like. Life throws in a million emergencies that need attention. But focus results are so astonishing they keep me going. And when you do it a few days in a row, the momentum can be amazing.

This week began with four focus hours cranking on the book Monday and Tuesday. The momentum shot me into Wednesday, the most productive work day of my life. I edited 30 pages of the book, wrote four proposals, three articles, and closed a business deal. Any one of those would usually take me a day.

Focus time sets the boundaries we need for thoughtful projects. In the next few chapters, we will explore some external support systems you can set up to help you create and maintain momentum in a given day.

Chapter 27
Making Space for Success
Controlling Clutter

*"If a cluttered desk is a sign of a
cluttered mind, just what does
an empty desk mean?"*

— Source Unknown

The terrible sibling of time chaos is space chaos. Clutter. Clutter kills our dreams. It fogs our vision. Cleverly disguised as temporary convenience ("I'll just put this here... for now") clutter undermines more progress than TV, soft-money campaign contributions, and badly designed web sites put together. Who can be a visionary leader, when vision is obscured by a stack of magazines waiting to be read, twenty signature pages to forgotten contracts, a file folder of "time-critical stuff" dated 4-17-1998, and an e-mail inbox the size of Texas?

For many of us, getting a handle on clutter is remarkably freeing. When you sit down at a clean desk, it's easy to start creating. A blank slate invites genius. Yet we've increased our clutter-generating ability to the point where we have physical clutter, mental clutter, schedule clutter and electronic clutter. And it does take its toll.

Clutter usually comes from deferring decisions

- We defer decisions about where to file things. "I don't have a place to put this piece of paper, so I'll let it sit on my desk until I deal."

- We defer decisions due to lack of information. "This project plan will wait in my inbox for Stacy to deliver the final info."

- We defer decisions due to lack of time to respond. "Marty sent me an e-mail? Excellent! No time to write back now, but I'll get to it later today."

Any one thing wouldn't be so bad, but the world throws information, requests, and interruptions at us so quickly that piles of stuff-to-do begin to build up. And once they begin, they're darned hard to rein back in. Today, eliminate some clutter from your life. Notice the effect this has on your feelings, your productivity level, and your ability to think clearly.

Eliminate a source of filing clutter

Look around your desk. Is there any pattern to the kind of stuff that's been living there for weeks? Are there a lot of bills? Client letters? Half-finished marketing plans? Identify one or two categories of paper and create files for them. Put the papers into files, and the files into your filing cabinet. Block out an hour in your schedule in the upcoming week to pull out the files and deal with the paperwork.

For the future, keep a stack of blank file folders within arm's reach. Toss in a labeling machine or a few sheets of peel-and-stick file folder labels. In the future, if something that needs it doesn't have a file, create the file then and there.

If you ever think, "this isn't important enough to create a whole file," then throw it out. If you can't, then it *is* important enough for a file. My solution: removable labels. It's easy to use a folder for a tiny project, knowing I can reuse it easily.

Eliminate some lack-of-information clutter

Create a file for "pending more information" documents. File the documents, and choose a time when you expect the information to be available. Block out a half-hour (or however long it will take) on your schedule to incorporate the information into the documents and send the documents off.

Review your "pending" file regularly. Throw out what's been taken care of, and follow up on things you're still expecting. The folder is its own reminder, so your brain doesn't need to waste time trying to track what's incomplete.

Eliminate some lack-of-time clutter

Identify three things you're putting off due to lack of time. Schedule them or cancel them, right now. If they aren't important enough to schedule, they aren't important enough to do. Eliminate them. Scream in agony as you do, but eliminate them nevertheless.

The basic pattern is the same: give your clutter a home and a deadline. Schedule the deadline, at which time you can throw away files that have expired or pull the files down and deal with them.

There are many types of clutter other than physical: we clutter our thoughts with irrelevant tangents; we clutter our time with non-fun, low-leverage activities; and we clutter our processes with bureaucracy and over-organization. And if you've been using computers for more than a year, you are probably discovering that there's a whole level of electronic clutter that mirrors our physical clutter.

For years, one of my major sources of clutter was the very "to do" lists that were supposed to keep me organized. In the next chapter, we'll master those once and for all.

Chapter 28
Organize Your Life with
Two "To Do" Lists

*"Plan your progress carefully; hour-by hour,
day-by-day, month-by-month. Organized
activity and maintained enthusiasm are the
wellsprings of your power."*

— *Paul J. Meyer*

It's been a pretty busy month, and I'm swamped with "to do" items. Post-it notes, scraps of paper, napkins, and dozens of scribbled "urgent" tasks are covering my desk. My Palm Pilot "to do" list terrifies me. Every night I pray, "Grant me freedom! Let my Palm's re-charger mysteriously run out of power." My prayers were answered in the book *The Organized Executive* by Stephanie Winston.

Stephanie suggests a method that's working great for me: Make a master "to do" list. Every single thing you have to do, no matter how big or small, goes into this list. Keep it in a permanent bound notebook, keep it with you at all times, and rather than scribbling a "to do" on a napkin, just record it in your

Master "To Do" list. Yes, you'll have thousands of items in your list. But it's okay, because the next step whittles it down to manageability.

Every morning, take out a clean white sheet of paper. Label it, Daily "To Do". Open your Master "To Do" list and copy nine (no more!) items from the Master "To Do" into your Daily list: three high priority items, three medium priority items, and three low priority items. You can copy whichever items seem appropriate on a given day. Then, run your day from the daily list.

At the end of the day, make sure any Daily items you may have scribbled down on that sheet are properly recorded in your Master List. Then toss your daily list and start fresh tomorrow.

If any items stay on your master list for longer than a few weeks, make the hard choice: tell yourself the Truth about whether you're actually going to do them. If you decide to do them, schedule them into your calendar. If not, cross them off your list.

This method provides a central place for "to dos", but a daily list that's manageable and relevant. I find the writing also causes me to browse my Master list much more often, which keeps me aware of which tasks I habitually procrastinate and which get done quickly.

Refine Your List by Context

You can expand this technique by keeping your master list sorted by person or place. For example, you'll write all "to dos" you can do in your office in one place. All running-errands "to dos" go on another page. All phone calls may be a third area of your list. Then when you're scanning your master list, if you know you'll be by a phone, you can go right to the "phone" section of your list. I keep an agenda page for my assistant and colleagues. When we meet, a quick turn to their page shows all the related "to dos", and everything gets covered with a moment's work.

Chapter 29
Dealing with Overwhelm
The Overwhelm Can Be Worse than the Backlog!

"We can lick gravity but sometimes the paperwork is overwhelming."

— Wernher Von Braun

Okay, you've blocked out focus time. You've cleared your clutter. Your task list is under control. But the simple fact remains: you have more to do than any human being can be expected to handle. You still feel overwhelmed. It's funny, when you think about it. The fact of overwhelm is bad enough, yet we compound it with a feeling that paralyzes and just makes things worse. The feeling is extra; why not be overwhelmed in fact, but at least feel great while we do it?

It's the feeling—not the overwhelm—that actually drains our energy. The feeling makes stress, which kills productivity. The less productive, the more work piles up. Bigger piles lead to more feelings of overwhelm, and the cycle repeats.

Once we've done everything we can to get organized, how can we conquer the draining feelings and go about getting things done?

Just do one thing at a time. Getting a lot done is really a matter of doing one thing at a time, whether or not you stress. If the problem is you've got a lot to do, turn the "lot" into a little by reducing the amount you're trying to do at once.

The next time you start to feel over committed, stop and take three deep breaths with your eyes closed. Take them from the diaphragm. Relax your shoulders. Relax the rest of your body. If it helps, get out of your chair and stretch a bit (I like to hang from the waist and touch my toes or do some other kind of inversion. That probably says something deep about my personality, but I'm not sure what.)

Next get out a piece of paper and list of everything you have to do—all the stuff that goes into the overwhelm. You can do this standing up, at your desk, or hanging upside down. Just write the whole list. Then decide which is most important to work on first. Set a time limit (if you don't have focus time scheduled that day, make some in the moment: "I'll work on this for two hours"), and promise yourself not even to look at the list until you've reached your time limit.

The work itself belongs in focus mode, so unplug the phone, shut down your e-mail program, close the door, and work solely on that one thing. When your time is up, pat yourself on the back, and move on to the next thing on your list.

The important thing is *not* finishing the task in two hours. What's important is making measurable progress you can feel good about. We tend to notice when we finish things, and we try for completion every chance we get. By blocking out a time limit instead of a completion milestone, you can feel good about making progress without needing to complete an entire project.

It also helps to keep a daily log of what you've accomplished. When I first started one, it seemed like some anal-compulsive habit from hell. But it makes a difference. At the end of the week, you can browse your log and realize that despite the mountains of Stuff To Be Done, you actually did far more than you thought you could. If you're like me and obsess on how much is left, rather than how much is done, a log is a nice way to chill by realizing how much progress you're really making.

Feelings of overwhelm happen when you bite off everything at once. The idea is to take life one thing at a time. Here's what makes this work:

* You write the list so your unconscious mind knows that focusing on one thing won't make you forget the other things.

* You choose your top priority thing to work on, rather than being interruption-driven.

* The time limit is also there for psychological reasons—when you know it's a defined span of time, you won't worry about "I'll never get to anything else." You know that an hour from now, you'll pull out the list and concentrate on the next thing.

Chapter 30
Operating at Your Peak
Sleep and Good Food are Underrated

"Drive your business, let not your business drive you."

— *Benjamin Franklin*

One of my clients was feeling under the weather. Motivation was down; stress was up. Instead of his usual optimistic, cheerful self, he'd become a melancholic gloom machine. Overall, a bad scene, and not one to set a good tone within the business—a CEO's mood can infect the entire company. The problem? He wasn't getting enough sleep, was working through his normal exercise time, and was making up the energy deficit with coffee during the day.

This is an all-too-common spiral. Too much work means too little sleep. Too little sleep means a drag on energy, less productivity, less creativity, and a sudden fondness for Starbucks. All that caffeine-induced energy makes it easy to work on into the night... and the whole thing starts over.

Unfortunately, chemically induced energy isn't enough. Our bodies and our minds need time to recharge. Sleep rests your body, and it also gives your mind time to explore and file everything that's happened during the day. The eighth hour of REM sleep, in fact, is where the most intense dreaming and creativity happen. Chemicals can keep your body awake, but your mind won't produce your best work unless you've had time to recharge.

While this has been known informally for years, an early 2004 study on sleep deprivation found that losing as little as a half hour of sleep can decrease people's creative problem-solving by up to 30%!

It's all too easy to let the occasional late night slide into a habit of not taking care of yourself. Breaking the downward spiral can be mentally difficult, but it's quite simple in practice: leave the office by 6:30 pm every night, even if stuff doesn't get done (the world won't end). Get a full night's sleep. Throw away your coffee maker. And start the day with a glass of water or juice. By the next week, you'll start feeling a lot better.

You're probably thinking, this sounds great in theory, but we couldn't do that and survive. You just don't understand how life is in a startup, competitive industry, tight schedule, high customer demand, *insert-favorite-excuse-here* situation.

Wrong-o. At least, if your employees do stuff that takes thought, "savings" from pushing people hard are usually short-term. You may need all-nighters in an emergency, but over time too little sleep impairs thinking ability. In a knowledge-intensive business, poor thinking can be deadly.

Startups often get away with a year or two of very intense work, but they risk burnout if it goes much longer. Burnout is unpredictable and hard to manage. You can easily ask a healthy workforce for occasional bursts of intense work. But when someone flips into burnout, they literally can't get started again. They stop caring, and often check out completely. At best, burnout is unmanageable, and it worst, it can be a total disaster.

A young workforce can take longer to burn out, but it still happens. Twenty-year olds can be hard on their bodies without feeling the effects as severely as we older folks. Several of my MBA classmates went full-tilt for a decade, and at least one had his first heart attack from stress and overwork (so said his doctor) in his mid-30s. In what world is that reasonable?

One way to promote health is lowering the workload. It means saying "No" to work that would be hurting people's health. It means building systems to save work, separating out the "must do" from the "we'd really like to do," and setting realistic client expectations if you're a service business.

But even if you don't lower the workload, sacrificing quality of life for short-term progress may be a fantasy. The basic math suggests that damaged immune systems still don't get the desired results. If someone loses three days to sickness that could have been avoided, that is equivalent to them having worked one hour less per day for an entire month (assuming ten-hour day, five-day workweeks)! It may be better to cut the extra hour off in the first place, and keep people in good health.

Scenario 1	Scenario 2
10 hour days	8.8 hour days
3 days sick	no days off
risk of spreading sickness	n/a
low quality of life	high quality of life

Both scenarios produce the same amount, but scenario 2 is a lot more fun for the person and the company.

The other way to manage workload is to genuinely work smart. "Work smart, not hard" is a great slogan, but most people haven't the foggiest idea what it means. Working smart means prioritizing ruthlessly, blocking out focus time for everyone who needs it, building systems to take care of repetitive tasks, and **most importantly, not instantly filling the newly freed time with more obligations and stresses**. One of our greatest insanities is that we make things quicker and faster with automation, but instead of enjoying the free time, we just fire half our workers and raise the bar for the other half.

Startups are especially bad. Most are run as pressure cookers. It's probably a misguided romantic notion that confuses movement with progress. A company I worked with closely took pride in their overwork, though an experienced project manager would instantly see the overwork came from poor scheduling, bad resource allocation, and a lack of attention to infrastructure that would have sped up later projects. The haste to get early contracts out the door sacrificed the opportunity to build systems for later productivity and later quality of life.

Because people think startups require sacrifice, they ask themselves, "How can we keep running the company the way we currently do, but avoid burnout?" The answer: you can't. If you're really enlightened, you might give out sabbaticals, which in one fell swoop loses the gains of several years' worth of overtime. That's the wrong question, and the wrong question always gives the wrong answer. The question to ask is, "How can we run the company in a healthful way?" The answer will depend on your company, your people, and your culture.

It's possible. My formerly caffeine-addicted CEO runs two companies staffed by people in their late-30s to fifties, and they don't need 100-hour weeks. But it takes care, planning, and constant attention to workload, infrastructure, and the like.

I'm sure that there are limited times—especially in startups—when deadlines and circumstances demand Herculean effort. But part of building a sustainable business is channeling effort into systems and structures that reduce the need for effort in the future. And even in startups, the gains from super-effort crunches are only gains in the short term. Most of them are more than made up for by decreased productivity, decreased creativity, which necessitates later rework, and time lost to sickness and required vacation.

Putting it into action:

This month, take steps to restore your life to an upward spiral.

- Commit to getting enough sleep every night for the next two weeks. Find out how that changes your outlook.

- Each day, substitute a glass of water or juice when you would normally drink coffee or soda. Learn to distinguish between caffeine energy and energy from health.

- Help your long-term balance by scheduling four weeks of vacation for next year. Do it now. Yes, I know that "there's no convenient time" or "emergencies happen." There's never a convenient time, and there will always be emergencies. Schedule your vacations and stick to them, realizing that the world around you will do its best to keep you from taking them.

About the Author

Stever Robbins is an executive coach, trainer, and speaker. He is President of Leadership Decisionworks, Inc., a leadership consulting firm located in Cambridge, Massachusetts.

An entrepreneur and technologist since the late 1970s, Stever has been a part of seven high tech start-ups and several IPOs. He led technology strategy and operations planning as COO for Building Blocks Interactive, and was a co-founder of early internet success story, FTP Software. As a project manager at Intuit, he led the development of the award-winning Quicken VISA Card.

Stever began training business executives as part of Harvard Business School's Leadership and Learning curriculum and has been an advisor and mentor to senior managers in several high-growth companies. Stever has an MBA from the Harvard Business School and a BS in Computer Sciences from MIT. He is a graduate of W. Edward Deming's Total Quality Management training program, and a Certified Executive Coach.

Stever Robbins is available for coaching, keynotes, and intensive half-day or full-day workshops. He can be reached at:

Leadership Decisionworks
(617) 354-1446
www.steverrobbins.com